HAIL
ENTREPRENEUR!

HAIL ENTREPRENEUR!

A Salute To An Endangered Species

By

EDWARD LOWE

May the strength

Of forging forward

Never be overcome

By the weakness of those

Who accept status quo

(FROM
"REFLECTIONS IN THE MILL POND"
VOL. X)

Also by Edward Lowe:

THE MAN WHO DISCOVERED THE GOLDEN CAT
(Autobiography)

REFLECTIONS IN THE MILL POND
(Poetry 10 volumes)

THE MAIN STREET JOURNAL
(Editor and Publisher)

ISBN # 0-8059-3659-9
Printed in the United States of America

First Printing

For more information or to order additional books,
please write:
Dorrance Publishing Co., Inc.
643 Smithfield Street
Pittsburgh, Pennsylvania 15222
U.S.A.

NOTE: *KITTY LITTER®* and *TIDY CAT®* are registered trade names of
THE GOLDEN CAT CORPORATION.

Dedication

Oh, Entrepreneur

*You have an unending desire to do something
And when you do something, you have an
Unending desire to do something else.*

*Your many urges, desires and impulses are like
The tide of the sea—always coming and going,
Thoughts like the waves instructed by the wind,*

*Dictating whether they are lazy swells, choppy whitecaps
Or thundering mountains—they cascade
Through your mind with uncontrolled direction.*

*It's not easy to give up; it's not easy to stay put;
It's not easy to go on riding wave after wave
Of this unsatisfied impulse; to move, to construct,
To dream, to do, but be instructed not to do.*

*The secret to satisfaction and success, then,
Must be dealt with very carefully by controlling
And adjusting the scales of deed to a delicate balance;
A balance that will be compatible with your own
Strengths and weaknesses.
But be wary that they do not become overbearing
To those who do not understand.*

*So pledge to the creed, Oh, Entrepreneur,
Bypass the negative, be patient with the structured,
Be passive with the limited, be understanding to
Those who are naive—
But never let your words, thoughts and deeds
Be smothered by those who cannot understand!*

**(Dedicated to my friends of old and my friends-to-be in the fellowship
of heroes whose entrepreneurial spirit sparks the flame of liberty.)**

Edward Lowe

TIME LINE

It Takes The Life Story Of The Man To
Develop The Lessons Of The Entrepreneur

THE STORY

1920	BORN July 10, 1920 in St. Paul Minn., the son of Henry Edward Lowe and Lulu Huber Lowe.
1925	MOVED to Marcellus, Mi (his mother's birthplace).
1939	GRADUATED from High School, Cassopolis, MI
1942	ENLISTED in the U.S. Navy, in the same U.S. Post Office where his father had enlisted in World War I (St. Joseph, MI).
1947	KITTY LITTER was born when he first packaged an absorbent clay to solve a problem for a neighbor whose cat box contained sawdust which tracked.
1957	RECORDED his first million dollars.
1967	INITIATED Purchase of BIG ROCK VALLEY acreage as the future base of THE EDWARD LOWE FOUNDATION.
1977	DEVELOPED the Granulated Technology which became the forerunner of another new industry for the use of inscecticide carriers in the agricultural field.
1987	**PUBLISHED through TOMORROW PRESS** ***"THE MAN WHO DISCOVERED THE GOLDEN CAT"*** **Life Story Of The Tom Sawyer Of Our Day** **Who Made a Hundred Million Dollars** **By Bringing The Cat In From The Cold.**
1990	EXPANDED his interests in many diversified entrepreneurial ventures.

HAIL ENTREPRENEUR!
Basic Survival Skills
by
Edward Lowe

CONTENTS

Foreword — Introducing the Entrepreneur's Entrepreneur

*Editor's Note: Edward Lowe's grandfather was "Grandpa Huber". Edward Lowe's grandson is "Austin". That's a span of 5 generations. In Grandpa Huber's mythical letters to his great, great grandson Austin, we get a long distance view of Edward Lowe, with perhaps a closer look at his achievements.

PORTRAIT OF MR. LOWE BY CARLO BENINATI

SECTION SIX

What Others May Think

POST SCRIPT

FOREWORD

INTRODUCING
THE ENTREPRENEUR'S ENTREPRENEUR

As this is being written, the headlines are crowded with the news that a wealthy man named Annenberg has given a half-billion dollars to the government for the purpose of improving our educational system. The nation is appropriately grateful. Mr. Annenberg and his accountants deserve all the thanks they are accredited. I am certain he is well-motivated.

I hope nobody, including Mr. Annenberg, will think me a spoilsport if I ask, "Will the $500 million do any good? Really? If so—how?"

Our schools are in a mess. Everybody knows that. Over half the kids drop out. In many cities there are police patrolling the school corridors to prevent rape, assault and murder. Drug pushers are in the playgrounds. If the teachers aren't on strike, many of them are incompetent or inept or already demoralized. The taxpayers are bleeding with the tax burden and there still isn't enough money to maintain the schools properly. There is no way taxpayers can get their money's worth.

The generous Annenberg grant may sadly turn out to be no more than planting seeds in the dry sands of the educational desert.

The ancient Jewish philosopher Maimonides gets a lot of credit for his wise teachings and one of them is that it is better to give a starving fellow a fishing pole than to throw him a few fish. In terms of today's crisis of education, we need to ask, "Who's going to teach that fellow how to fish?"

Ed Lowe has the answer to that question.

Sometimes money—even a lot of it—won't make a rusty engine operate smoothly. In the light of Annenberg's splendid gift we must ask ourselves: will the schoolchildren have enough nutrition to learn well? Will they have enough family love to want to learn? Will the teachers be adequately educated and sufficiently motivated to teach the kids? Will there be enough school buildings and classrooms? Will the taxpayers be able to support the school system?

Now turn these penetrating questions toward the economy itself. Our economic feet are dragging. The national debt is frightening. Our rate of growth is falling drastically behind. The Gross National Product is in a slump.

Many people, mostly politicians, believe the answer is for the government to pump more money into the system—create WPA-type jobs, dole out government grants and other entitlements. The problem here is that the government has no money except what it takes from us in the form of taxes. You can't borrow from Peter to pay Peter although we keep trying.

The additional problem is that government-financed "jobs" are not true wealth-creating jobs which widen the tax base. They are artificial creations which add to the national debt, heighten inflation and deter an authentic revival of the economy.

Ed Lowe's answer is to start at the beginning. Get down to basics. What our economy needs now is not "free" fish. Not even the gift of a fishing pole. It needs to be taught how to fish!

Ed Lowe's formula starts with Small Business because it is the foundation for Big Business. His answer starts with the Entrepreneur who is the growth cell for Small Business. His answer starts with sharing the wisdom his lifetime has collected. In this book, through words and pictures, case histories, examples and plain-talking expositions, Edward Lowe tells the reader: IT CAN BE DONE. I KNOW BECAUSE I DID IT. And herein he tells exactly how he did it, so that you can do it, too.

In his first book, *"The Man Who Discovered The Golden Cat,"* Ed related the entertaining story of his life—what made him the person he turned out to be. In this book he tells you what he has learned along the way. He

xiv

says, "I figure that when a man spends a lifetime learning things, he should be able to share that learning if he can find those who want to learn."

At last count there were 2,437,618 books on "How To Succeed." (Don't pay any attention to that figure, I just made it up to impress you with the fact there are a bunch of such "Success" books.) This book is not a "Success" book. (O, you might count "How To Be A Successful Failure" a Success book, until you realize that Ed wrote it with his tongue-in-cheek, to amuse you as well as enlighten you.)

No, this is not a success book. Ed Lowe has raised the frightening warning that "The Entrepreneur is an endangered species". He firmly believes, as you should believe, that the dangers that beset the small owner-operated independent business are a threat to American free enterprise as a whole. This book of his is a book of survival skills. It must be read between the lines.

You'll see that this is a book about "How To Survive".

"You can't succeed without surviving," Ed Lowe tells us. "And if you survive in this day and age maybe you've got a chance to be a success."

As you will see, as the book develops, it "shares" the wit and wisdom of this man who brought the cat in from the cold, and is now turning waste into worthwhile recyclable granules. His half-century of entrepreneurial genius is being capsulated in some 30 chapters, ranging from economics to history to philosophy—all pertaining to the day-to-day operations of the entrepreneur.

"This is not a professorial dissertation," Ed says, "because I am not a professor. If ever I had any secrets, they are secrets no longer, because entrepreneurs can read it. It could save them a lot of trouble. It might even make the difference between striking gold...or striking out."

A principal dictum of Ed Lowe's survival credo is "Make a lot of love and have fun together."

He wrote this book so that you, hopefully, could make progress in your chosen path. And in reading it, certainly have fun.

Burr McCloskey
Editor

SECTION ONE

FAILURE OR SUCCESS?

Dear Reader,

   It's really up to you to make up your mind—do you sincerely want to succeed, or are you prepared to fail? Let's look at the choices.

   To start with, if you intend to fail, my advice is: <u>do it right. Go for it big time.</u>

THE
ILLUSTRATED MANUAL
OF SCIENTIFIC RULES
ON

HOW
TO BE A
SUCCESSFUL
FAILURE

"Failure ain't easy" — TIME Magazine
"It takes determination to fail" — FORTUNE
"There's nothing worse than a half-assed failure" — Karl Marx

Endorsed by the U.S. BANKRUPTCY COURT

INTRODUCTION

GET YOURSELF IN A "HAPPY FAILURE MOOD"

*Believe!—
It's all a matter
of luck,
anyway...*

Instructions for Beginners

(1) If you want to be a sloppy failure
  - Go to Las Vegas
  - Become a lush
  - Rob a bank

(2) If you want to fail in a high-style professional way _read these rules_

(3) It's _not_ bad to be a failure. It's _bad_ to be a bad failure

APPLYING

RULE #1

FOR A LOAN

PRESIDENT

- [ ] There's no need to be too formal

- [ ] Call the president by his first name *(better yet, call him "Chuck" or "Lefty")*

- [ ] Don't bother about a business plan

- [ ] Complain about the many NSF checks you get

- [ ] Ask the president's daughter for a date

- [ ] Tell a few funny jokes *(loudly)*

- [ ] Sprinkle in a few four letter words

DON'T GET [RULE #2] STUCK WITH ANY ONE PLAN

- ☐ Write a great Business Plan today

- ☐ Write another one tomorrow

- ☐ Disregard **both** of them the next day

- ☐ Plans destroy your flexibility

DO IT

RULE #3

TOMORROW

- ☐ Never do today what you can put off till tomorrow

- ☐ Procrastination gives extra time for others to screw it up

- ☐ If you don't do it now, you won't regret doing it wrong

- ☐ Delay it—haste makes waste

- ☐ It will keep in the "Procrastination Drawer"

DO IT

ALL YOURSELF

☐ To heck with teamwork

☐ Take full responsibility

☐ Get up early and open up

☐ Sweep up, open the mail

☐ Hide the checks (cash a few)

☐ TRUST ABSOLUTELY NOBODY

IGNORE

RULE # 5

PROFIT & LOSS

☐ It's all a gamble anyway!

☐ Forget this is a capi-talistic system

☐ Pay no attention to cash flow

☐ GO BROKE
   WITH A BIG
   BANG!

DON'T GIVE | RULE #6 |

YOURSELF A PAY CHECK

- ☐ Keep borrowing from yourself

- ☐ Make your family suffer, be frugal but not for yourself

- ☐ Feed the business— starve yourself

- ☐ Dig yourself deeper and deeper into debt— which *(fortunately)* leads to better failure

RULE #7

NO PONDERING ALLOWED

☐ Let your mind skip around like a jackrabbit

☐ Never settle down and think it over

☐ Enjoy a chronic state of confusion

☐ Avoid serious reflection about anything

SLOW DOWN | RULE #8
WHEN THINGS ARE UP

- ☐ When things are busy, take time off to count your money

- ☐ If orders are coming in, take a break

- ☐ Stay home, don't put any "rubber on the road"

- ☐ Do your best to be negative

NOBODY ELSE IS NO. 1

RULE # 9

☐ Monopolize the limelight

☐ Give no respect to anybody else

☐ Be as obnoxious as possible

☐ Brag about yourself—refer to "ME" a lot

PUT ROUND PEGS IN SQUARE HOLES

RULE #10

- ☐ Hire people who just don't fit

- ☐ Undertake projects that are not thought through

- ☐ Lots of square holes & round pegs = Failure

DON'T

RULE # 11

SHARE THE GOOD TIMES

- ☐ Don't give credit to anyone else

- ☐ Hog all the glory for yourself

- ☐ Be a real Simon LeGree—hog the profits!

- ☐ Life is a holiday

INSIST

ON YOUR OWN
WAY

☐ Don't consider anyone else's advice

☐ No open door to your office

☐ Ignore other's suggestions

☐ To heck with the team theory

SHARE

RULE # 13

NO CREDIT

☐ Nobody else has helped you

☐ The team members are just "lackeys"

☐ If you're not the hero—who is?

☐ There's only one Big Shot—YOU

BE SHODDY

RULE #14

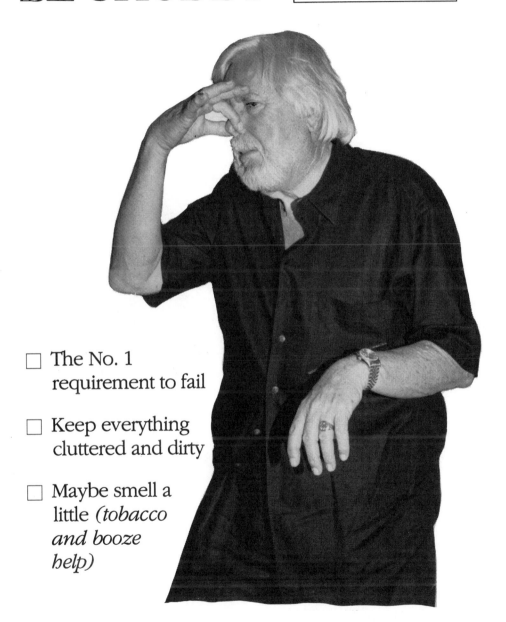

- ☐ The No. 1 requirement to fail

- ☐ Keep everything cluttered and dirty

- ☐ Maybe smell a little *(tobacco and booze help)*

PAY NO ATTENTION TO LITTLE THINGS

RULE # 15

KITCHEN MATCHES

NO MATCHES

☐ Details are just a headache

☐ Never grease the little parts

☐ BIG THINGS are what count

☐ Ignore the little things, they ignore you

FORGET

RULE # 16

ABOUT LOVE & FUN

☐ Don't love your mission & your mates

☐ Don't have fun doing your thing

☐ Do be a heartless person

☐ Who needs love anyway?

19

CONCENTRATE ON FAILING

RULE # 17

☐ Keep your mind on a negative focus

☐ Always pooh-pooh the optimistic view

☐ It takes real determination to fail

☐ Know in your heart that you're a failure

☐ Fail with purpose

BELIEVE

RULE # 18

THESE RULES

GEE, I'M SO GLAD TO BE A LOSER. IT'S LESS WORK THAN YOU THINK.

☐ Be enthusiastic about losing

☐ Accept "the inevitable"

☐ Say "I didn't deserve to succeed"

☐ It's less work to lose

You've Earned Your Diploma!

Official Dishonorable Degree

MASTER OF FAILURE

◇◇◇◇◇◇◇◇◇◇◇

The undersigned is hereby designated as an

ACCREDITED FAILED PERSON

Entitled to all the penalties and fines attached thereto

USA   Bankruptcy
          Referee   ——————————————
                                        sign here

Guaranteed to be a

PROFESSIONAL FAILURE

(No money back if this claim is ever forfeited.)

PLEASE NOTE!

In keeping with his lifetime practice based on the philosophy, "If you can't get anybody else to do it, do it yourself", Mr. Edward Lowe has artfully served as the model for these enlightening lessons on how to be a successful failure. If one or any of the photographs for which Mr. Lowe was the model should seem exaggerated, that was exactly the intention.

The Editor

ℒETTER TO AUSTIN

Hello, young fellow—how's your luck today? I want to talk to you about that. A lot of folks—some bright ones and some not-so-bright—say this about your Grandpa Lowe—they say that he was "lucky".

I've tried to understand what that signifies. I suspect it means that he just "fell into it", and really doesn't deserve all the good fortune he has earned the hard way. They must think that his discovery of Kitty Litter was just a lucky accident and that he made it big out of sheer luck.

Now, my Grandson Eddie is the first to admit that he has enjoyed good fortune. He's inclined to think that it was lucky he got home that day when his neighbor came over to ask for something for her cat box.

Well, I'm here to say that the harder Eddie worked, the luckier he got. There's no way you can blame his success on blind luck. I'll tell you something about Lady Luck, Austin—you can't count on luck in the long run. If that's all you've got, your luck is sure to run out.

With my Eddie, please stand informed that he worked and he worked and then he worked some more to produce a better product in better ways, sell it and promote it and distribute it in ever-improving ways. He had some good breaks and he also had some bad breaks. He well-deserved every good thing that ever came his way.

Now it's true he doesn't claim all the credit for what he's achieved. He gives ample credit to the people who helped him along the way. And most of all—above everything else—he knows that Divine Guidance was mainly responsible.

And that's my lesson for you, Austin—*don't ever confuse God with Lady Luck.*

Love ya

Grandpa Huber

AVOIDING FAILURE

By Reversing The Rules On How To Fail

BASIC PRINCIPLES

▶ Find out what the fellow who failed did
—and don't do it

▶ Remember that failure is a common disease
—don't catch it

▶ Don't let the distractions of failure lure you away from success
—stay on track

▶ Get yourself into the habit of succeeding
—and don't break the habit

▶ Be proud of your successful achievements
—and be ashamed of screwing up

TO GET FINANCIAL HELP

RULE # 1

- Consider how *you* would regard anybody asking you for a loan, and act accordingly

- Assemble your business plan and records to amply justify the sum you are requesting

- Let your dress and your deportment reflect your credibility

- Don't whine, plead, beg or boast—let the facts speak for themselves

- Be prepared and eager to answer all appropriate questions and inquiries

- Muster as many references as possible to support your good standing

- Review the Boy Scout pledge

FOLLOW YOUR PLAN

RULE # 2

■ Design your business plan based on sound basic principles

■ Understand that your plan establishes your business goals and direction

■ Know which essential principles and procedures must be followed—if not, ask and find out

■ Define which areas are open for amendment if conditions change

■ Treat your business plan as the U.S. regards the U.S. Constitution

TOMORROW NEVER COMES

RULE # 3

- Set firm but realizable time tables for specific jobs, projects and quotas

- Then treat those deadlines almost as sacred pledges

- Remember that when one deadline is violated, all deadlines in sequence are messed up

- If you keep on schedule, that record will be the barometer of your business health

- Believe that efficiency begins and ends with your fidelity to your time tables

- Develop a critical path, then stay on it

NO MAN IS AN ISLAND

RULE # 4

■ Your first partnership is with your own conscience so evaluate yourself often

■ Then you are involved in teamwork with any and all serving your business—especially your customers

■ Let everyone involved feel that you respect and value their collaboration

■ Delegate all possible responsibilities to the members of your team

■ Delegate everything except the leadership of the team—Remember that's *your* responsibility

■ Trust your team members until and unless they violate that trust

KEEP YOUR EYE ON THE SCORE

RULE # 5

- Don't entertain yourself with "blue sky" hopes and illusions

- Remember that operating cash on hand is the bloodline of your company

- Your profit margins are what keep the game going

- It's not a sin to make a profit—it's a sin to fall on your face

- P&L is the scoreboard for winning or losing

PUT YOURSELF ON PAYROLL

RULE # 6

- Please remember you are not running a charitable institution

- You are managing an authentic business, and are not on welfare

- Your first obligation is to keep the "boss" solvent—that's **yourself**

- When you donate time and sacrifice your own interests, you're cheating on someone

- If you can't pay yourself, it won't be long before you can't pay anyone

TAKE TIME TO THINK

RULE # 7

- Never get so busy you don't know what is going on

- Never be so occupied with Today that you forget about Tomorrow

- Always give your mind a "Time Out" to look ahead

- Stand off on the sideline and reflect on the total scene

- Raise your mind's sights above the dust of the battle. Now and then thank somebody for yesterday

GO WITH THE FLOW

RULE # 8

- ■ Be closely aware of the rhythm and the tempo of your operation

- ■ Watch your priorities closely and don't get them confused

- ■ Keep pace with whatever is on the front burner

- ■ Prepare ahead for the "busy season"

- ■ Don't relax until the pressure is off—be well-balanced, remember the teeter totter

SHARE THE LIMELIGHT

RULE # 9

- When production is the pressure point, give a salute to the producers

- When sales are the critical thing, honor the sales staff

- If quality improvement is the key, encourage the researchers

- Keep *your* head at all times, creating a stable atmosphere

- As a general rule, it's better to know than guess

PICK YOUR TEAM WISELY

RULE # 10

- Don't let personal favoritism pick your personnel

- Try not to let persuasive "fast talkers" fool you about their individual attributes

- Let your hiring decisions and policy be based on proven merits

- Know the job's requirements first and then pick people to match

- Don't adjust the job to accommodate people you'd like to hire

- As a general rule, left-handers can't write right-handed

SPREAD THE GOOD WORD

RULE # 11

- When things are going well, pass the word around

- Let the whole team share the glory when records are broken

- Know that company loyalty depends on how much the team bonds with the company

- Keep your own ego in tow—so the team knows you appreciate its efforts

- Never let the "rat race" destroy your personal humanity

- As the song says, "The good news is that the bad news was wrong"

APPEARANCES DO COUNT

RULE # 12

■ Note that a screwed-up facility does screwed-up work

■ Handsome is as handsome does—so keep *yourself* looking sharp

■ The world judges you and your company on how you look

■ If the package is badly wrapped, nobody will bother to open it

THINK SMALL

RULE # 13

- The world is one real BIG THING containing a countless number of wee LITTLE THINGS

- Handling those little details is the only way to get a handle on the Big Things

- You must repair the defective small parts before the big ones fall to pieces

- Never get too big for your britches, or too big to watch out for the tiny details

MAKE LOVE, HAVE FUN

RULE # 14

- Hard work and no fun makes Jack a dull boy—and doesn't make too much "jack" anyway

- Good hard work and well-earned success should not rule out the Good Life

- Loving your family and your friends makes the work all the more enjoyable

- Doing what you want to do and doing it well will grant you plenty of fun

- A good temper and a happy mood will show up in your bank account

KEEP POSSESSION OF THE BALL

RULE # 15

- The "ball" is your company's success

- The question is not *what* to do, but *how* to best do it

- Your success will be measured by the quotas you set for yourself and the quotas you meet

- Focus on success—it is a magnet that will draw you to it

- You can't win the game without the ball *(Ask the coach)*

LETTER TO AUSTIN

Hey Buddy! I figure you're old enough now for me to explain something to you about your Grandpa Lowe. It's kinda confidential but I know you'll understand. Some folks think it's sort of peculiar.

The plain fact is—he writes poems. You probably knew that. It's a fact, and he not only writes'em, but every Christmas he gets them printed up in a book and sends 'em to his friends.

Now you may wonder how come a practical-minded man like your grandfather comes by this instinct and talent to write poetry? Some folks do wonder about it. OK, that's what I want to explain to you...

Here's the answer, Austin—there's two sides to every coin!

There's heads, and there's tails. This applies to a person, too. There's always more to a body than meets the eye.

This is especially true of a person like your Grandpa who happens to be especially creative. That sort of person has a work-side and a play-side. There's serious-side and a fun-side. There's a down-to-business side and a side that wants to write poetry. That creative nature wants to keep producing new things and new words in new ways—just like a healthy hen has to keep on laying eggs.

Poetry is a way of looking at things in life in an out-of-the-ordinary way. It sheds a new light on everyday affairs.

This applies to you, little fellow. You can write your poetry in your own way and your own style. It may be in music or in dance or carving wood statues. Whatever way your talent takes you, so keep yourself in balance, you don't dare forget the other side.

That's what they mean when they say, "Be sure to pick a few posies along the way." When both sides of you are in full gear, you're certain to be a well-balanced person. Your teeter-totter will be well balanced in the playground of life.

Love ya

Grandpa Huber

*I know
because
I am one!*

HOW I DID IT!

The Shameless Confessions of an Entrepreneur who is successful

by Edward Lowe

*The man
who is glad to show you how
YOU can do it too!*

SOME INSIDE REVELATIONS
(FOR YOUR BENEFIT)

1　The Decision

2　Response

3　The Support Team

4　Trusting Your Instincts

5　Vision

6　Self-Control

7　Defense From Competition

8　Promoting Your Product

9　Policy On Prices

10　The Personal Approach

11　Quality Control Outside

12　Packaging

I DID IT MY WAY

Edward Lowe's Personal Story

THE DECISION

The very first thing I did was to make the decision to be independent. It was a tough decision to make, and I didn't then understand the long-range ramifications of the act. *I decided to be independent from my father.* We just didn't get along.

He didn't like it, and he penalized me for making the decision. My dad was an entrepreneur. I inherited from him that inbred entrepreneurial urge to be self-centered. His reaction to my move put a knot in my stomach. He refused to give me much, if any, support but I was motivated to go it on my own, breaking away from my father's line of business.

One decision leads to many others. This next one was subordinate but it was a major decision—*in which direction would my independence take me?*

When you come to a crossroads in your life, it's surprising how many choices you seem to have. I'd had some experience, real money-making experience, and I was offered the opportunity to sell heavy machinery. There was good money to be made in that direction and I had proven that I could possibly make out in that field.

On the other hand, I was already testing the possibility of *"Kitty Litter"*. Its future was problematical but it looked more interesting to me. It looked to be more fun, more stimulating than the greasy atmosphere of machinery sales. I liked the human contact that goes along with everyday consumer products and giving people something they enjoyed, that made their lives a little better.

It's hard to measure, but your motivation counts a lot when you're up against a decision that can change your life. The *"fun"* angle, meaning the satisfaction I could garner from dealing with people, outweighed the *"risk"* factor.

So it was that cats became part of my life. And, I must admit it, I became part of the life of millions of cat owners. I have never once regretted that decision.

RESPONSE

I mentioned "risk". People attach that label to entrepreneurs a great deal. It's partly justified, but it really doesn't justify calling entrepreneurs "gamblers" or wild-eyed speculators. The key thing is that when your futures aren't all cut-and-dried, of course there is uncertainty in the road you take. There's risk every time you take a step in the dark—you could fall into a hole.

The first thing you do, and I did it, after making a decision, is to start looking for solid ground—try to take the risk out of the journey you're about to make.

You've got a product or a service and you need to find out whether there is any consumer appetite for it. You've to to judge the need and measure the response. Then if things look promising—*go for it!*

I knew I had *some* potential in Kitty Litter, starting with my neighbor Kay Draper and her positive response to it. But that wasn't enough to fortify my real belief in it. I needed a wider, more objective reaction.

So I managed to place it in the Davenport Pet Shop in South Bend. Mr. Davenport at first turned it down because he couldn't believe that anybody would pay that much for it. What could I do? I guess some "risk" was involved. *I gave it to him.* "If you sell it", I told him, "Let me know and I'll bring you another order." That triggered some healthy action. He did sell it and I did bring him more.

I kept bagging it, had some labels printed, and went looking for other pet shops.

You throw a pebble into a pond and it sends out rings and ripples from its point of impact. Marketing is like that. *I wanted a wider ripple.* The next thing I did was approach the sponsors of a cat show. It made sense to me that those folks who thought enough about cats to put them in shows, or go to such exhibits, would also be interested in a new product for in-house cat hygiene.

I proposed to the show's sponsor that I would furnish the cat boxes, filler and clean the cages, if they'd give me a booth and let me advertise my stuff. We made a deal.

You see, I knew my product. I knew that the clay I used would absorb the liquid and that once absorbed the odor would be nullified. Cat shows up until then were really *odoriferous* environments! Not only were the exhibitors grateful but so were the guests—and the word was passed around—Kitty Litter had worked wonders!

Then I went on the road. The oldtime pioneer "Mountain Men" (America's first entrepreneurs) knew how to track wild game, and Lesson No. One was *"Don't let the trail get cold!"* By this time I had a pretty good notion that I had a live one by the tail (no pun intended). From that time on, I put rubber on the road. I went to Chicago and from there to Milwaukee. After that it was St. Paul and on and on. Across the country east and west, north and south, I set up 75 distributing points.

Consumer response, when it comes, is like hooking a fish. The line tugs and then, O boy!—*you've got to pull it in.*

THE SUPPORT TEAM

There comes that critical moment when you know darned well you have got yourself a load of business opportunities *which you absolutely cannot lift by yourself.* You know you need help. It wasn't long before I faced that need.

It isn't as simple as it sounds. You've got to analyze exactly what kind of a work force is essential at this time. Once you know the classifications and the types you need, you've got to attract them. You have to find the support team that's right for you at this important stage of development, workers who want to do what needs to be done—and know how to do it. Then ask yourself "Am I willing to risk that load? Can I afford them?"

Ability is essential, of course. Willingness is a big item. But the biggest of all, I think, is *loyalty.* I had to have a loyal core to my support group. I was on the road most of the time; I had no watch dog. My costs and margins were so sensitive that if I couldn't trust the team I could go busted at any time. I was at the cutting edge of success or failure.

Loyalty is a two-way street. It starts with the entrepreneur. You are the hub of the wheel. I had to recognize the right help when I found them. And they had to know that I recognized *them,* appreciated their loyalty and was as fair as I could be in my relations with them. Bob, Denny and Mrs. Egmer... they were the charter group of what was later to become a payroll of over seven hundred people. I cannot forget their loyalty and the love they gave me. Denny was a huge sort of simple man, and when I visited him at the hospital his last words to me touched my heart. Denny mostly carried bags of Kitty Litter to the bin. His last words were, *"I'd like to carry one more bag to the bin."*

Once I got in motion, traveling across country, Bob Follett was in charge of operating affairs around our plant, and Mrs. Egmer was handling cash flow details. They were great supporters in my company's early days of formation. And of course, Denny carried the bags to the bin.

People have said that I was fair with my employees. I think my employees would back that up. I tried my best to be fair. I may even have tried too much. If anything, I tended to yield, to hold off from discharging a person who might have needed discharging. I tended to give just a little more than prevailing terms called for. But something in me kept me from going around and softsoaping everybody like a politician running in a popularity contest. If they liked me and working for me, it had to come from the heart, not from softsoaping... I guess it paid off in the long run. I now know that it did.

TRUSTING YOUR INSTINCTS

By this time, I was beginning to think and act like a trueblue entrepreneur. A free enterprise businessman, strictly on his own, doesn't automatically fill the entrepreneur's boots. *He has to grow into them.* I was growing *fast!*

You can't learn it all from books (even books like this one.) There aren't enough hours in the day to do a lot of reading, anyway. So where do you get your guidelines? A lot more than you might think has to come instinctively—from deep inside, plus finding a mentor here and there.

Instinct is the thing, your "gut feeling". You have to trust yourself in a pinch. Believe me, that's a very brave thing to do when you're young, all alone and running in high gear where a bad move can cause a smash-up.

First off, I had the impulse to *innovate.* All basic entrepreneurs have this faculty. It begins with imagination and it comes to the fore in the itch to change, to adapt, to work out improvements in anything and everything whatever. This isn't something you have to force yourself to do. You can't help it. All entrepreneurs have it. Shut me up in a closet for twenty minutes and I will innovate *something.* It might be a cup with two handles for right and left hands. It might be a three-

way mirror which shows you from different angles—unlike the conventional view. It might be numbering sheets of toilet paper so little kids can learn how to count and not waste it.

This is not to say that every cup with two handles is a magic money-maker. But it is to say that you've got to give your gift for innovation a free rein. *Don't cramp your gut feelings!* Learn to look inside yourself for answers when there aren't any answers in plain view. When you've got to make a critical decision, don't ignore the soundings you get from your inner self. If you can't trust yourself, who is going to trust *you?* (Ponder a bunch and follow a hunch.)

VISION

You know what a crow's nest is? That's where the look-out on a sailing ship is located on the highest mast the ship has. *The entrepreneur is always posted in his crow's nest.*

He is always on the look-out. "Vision" is his best insurance against failure.

A reporter once asked Coach Landry of the Dallas Cowboys, "Why don't you get excited when a play is being executed? You seem so calm and collected." And the coach replied, "It's because I'm thinking about the *next* play, the play-to come, and my mind isn't on this one." That's vision at work.

You've got to look ahead. "Funnel vision" is a pet model of

mine, showing how you can extend your vision simply by having a *far-out attitude* with a field of observation more expanded than the ordinary. *In my beginning days I had to look out for cats.*

My home base of Cassopolis and South Bend wasn't the only territory in the United States that featured pet cats. I climbed up in my crow's nest and took a visionary look around to see where my future was. (My advice to start-up entrepreneurs is to look far enough ahead and you're bound to see yourself down the road somewhere.)

At the time, the National Association of Veterinarians said there were twenty-three million cats in the country. What proportion of them made my best marketing target?

It didn't take a lot of brainwork to figure that pet cats were my best customers and that a lot of that total were indeed pet cats. I analyzed it this way: let's figure that some 50% of them were farm cats, outdoor cats or just wild strays. They used to be called alley cats. (I figure that not only did I introduce a new word, *"Kitty Litter"* into the language, I also wiped out an old term, *"alley cat"*. You win some and you lose some.)

My guess was that the other 50% had some sort of a home. Somebody cared for them. And of these maybe half of them were pedigreed cats.

They might have to be put out at night but they did have a home. I was interested in those cat owners who were willing to pay 69¢ for five pounds of my litter in order to keep their cats in the house overnight in safety.

"Vision" is not a simple matter of eyesight. You see with your *mind*. That's where your crow's nest is— *inside your mind*. Climb it and take a good look. That's what I was doing.

I didn't go to any million-dollar consultants. I estimated my special target market as being some *two and one-half million cats*. That was the vision that kept me going, kept me innovating, kept me putting rubber on the road. My goal was to sell each cat-lover one 5 lb. bag a month. That amounted to 5x2.5 million—*BIG TIME!*

That's my advice to any young eager entrepreneur—*COUNT YOUR CATS!* Whatever your business or whatever the product, there are cats to be counted in one form or another. And if you count your cats, you're bound to find kittens.

It was easy for me to deduce that my target cats were principally in metropolitan areas, so I located those cities where the cat shows would be. I pinpointed my strategy to open a distributor in each of those areas on a national basis. There are a couple of good laws in this regard. The old one is "If it ain't broke, don't fix it", and my new one, as my history demonstrates, is *"If it's working well keep it working."*

SELF CONTROL

Now I started suffering from some growing pains. It happens to all of us in a successful business and the newcomers must be prepared for it. A little bit of success tends to go to your head. You climbed a little hill and now you think you can take Mount Everest. You're so tickled with your instinct for innovation that you're ready to re-invent the wheel. This means pondering time is in order.

When you're driving a good team of horses, you don't dare let them get out of hand. *Control is the order of the day,* and *self-control* is the major issue. Entrepreneurs have to put up with a lot of distractions.

My eyes moved off the ball. My itch to create new projects took over. It's an occupational disease that comes with the territory. Watch out for it. I went through a period of deviation. I started experimenting with just about everything under the sun—from firewood to birdseed to pet shops. There was some virtue in all of them, but they were not for me at the time and it cost me to get wise about them. I was putting so much effort into things I had no business fooling with, I was ignoring which fire was hot. *That was the cat box filler fire.* I had to learn what every entrepreneur has to learn—*PUMP YOUR BELLOWS ON THE FIRE THAT'S HOT!*

You've got to learn *control.* The business graveyard is full of business failures that simply lost control.

They weren't run over by competition or bad luck. They committed a form of self-destruction by losing control, forgetting to act smart, then blaming it on hard luck or something else.

Control the team, control the market strategy, and most of all control *yourself*—keep your eye on the ball. Yes, there is the factor of good fortune and lucky breaks. I heard a fellow say, "The harder I work, the luckier I get." The thing is, you can't count on luck—you have no control, over it. There's the matter of Divine Guidance, too, but that's in God's hands, not in yours.

Another thing, don't surrender your control to outsiders. Once you do that, the spirit of independent entrepreneurship is killed. You can take advice from a knowledgeable outsider, but *not* control. The entrepreneur has to run his own shop. That's the kind of an animal he or she is. Approach management very carefully. *Be the leader.*

DEFENSE FROM COMPETITION

Being first in the field draws a lot of fire. The thing that woke me up and got me off dead-center was the arrival of competition. While you resent it when it happens, in time you realize that the pressure of competing firms is the action that tempers American steel. I'm not denying that it smarts—especially when they try underhanded tactics. But I must say this—my competition kept me sharp and taught me many things. I had not only my foot in the door but also my leg!

If you strike oil, you can't be surprised to wake up to find oil wells all around you. It happened to me and it woke me up. It forced me to be alert—to climb up the old crow's nest and stay on the look-out. Beware of manageritis.

Competition comes in all guises. There's price competition. Advertising competition. Packaging and distribution was highly competitive on every front. Those critics who think my success was just plain luck don't give me credit for keeping ahead of the strongest corporate competitors in American commerce.

Once we got into the grocery field, the competition was a lot fiercer than in the pet shops. Shelf space in the supermarkets is like getting a box seat at the Rose Bowl. You have to protect yourself on all sides, and of course your main defense is the loyalty of your customers, which had always been based on the cat.

The problem is that you can't reward that loyalty if you can't get through the pipe lines to supply your customers. I knew I was up against the Big Boys now and that it wasn't any church picnic or local baseball game. I had to enlarge my team. I had to go "pro".

This led to one of my greatest creations. I'm proud of it but that's not why I'm making a point of it. I *had to develop a national sales organization.* Sooner or later, once a young company spreads its wings, it *must* create or find or adapt a selling system to take it into the national marketplace. Every entrepreneur has to look for opportunities to build up forces beyond his own jurisdiction.

When he can find forces going his way they can prove to be an immense value, perhaps the saving value, of his marketing momentum. I put together a national brokerage group. How did I do it? *I recognized the entrepreneur's spirit that motivated key brokers.* I went after them and they responded. They are loyal to me to this day. I paid attention to them. I invested in them. The broker is not like an in-house salesman. The broker takes orders and is paid commissions on the orders he takes. He lives on his earnings. My broker organization was a network of entrepreneurs and became my main offensive line against the competition.

PROMOTING YOUR PRODUCT

Jimmy Cagney, a fine actor, once told his formula for good acting. He said, "You walk on stage (or in front of the camera) and you look the fellow (whoever he may be) in the eye. *Then you tell the truth.*"

Think about it. In that simple statement *you have the secret of advertising.* It's the Golden Rule in practice. Don't tell your public anything you don't believe yourself.

At the beginning, your advertising is an announcement that you're in business and what you are offering. My first little ad in Better Homes and Gardens brought me an avalanche of returns. Once you've pulled that trigger, you move into another stage of advertising—*your ads have to stand up to the ultimate truth*. If you say (as I did) that your product controls odor and it doesn't—then your ads aren't worth a plugged nickel.

Your mission is to tell the buying public how your product will help them, and tell them honestly. You can't advertise by saying, "Buy this because it will help us pay for this ad." That reminds me of a sign I saw in a little old restaurant, *"Come on in and eat before we both starve."* We always put customer benefits first and foremost.

Do you know the best way to identify the benefits of your product (whatever it may be?) You have to put yourself in your customer's shoes. What does the customer want? What does the customer need? What will the customer be glad to get? Once you've taken this inventory, you'll be surprised at the number of benefits you can uncover and rightly spotlight in your ads. I did that with Kitty Litter and brought out all the customer benefits we could find. It absorbs. It deodorizes and is trackless. It is dust-free. What we were telling our customers was: *Buy our product and your cat's life will be better and so will yours.*

We knew we were best in the field, but we weren't content just to be a little better than our competitors. We had to be better than *ourselves*. We had to keep on bettering ourselves in a policy of extended research and continuous improvement. Our slogan was *"Make the best better."*

Advertising is like the sail on the ship. The taller the sail, the heavier the keel must be; otherwise it tips over.

The keel for our advertising was our research. I had to put in a department with trained people to watch cats and study their behavior. I had to see that we learned how to precisely regulate the size of our granules. We demonstrated how dust was injurious to cat's eyes, working with vets all across the country. (I was the only catbox filler company to be granted an award from them.)

Our advertising kept us in the lead of all the competitors, but our keel kept us in steady balance. We never got down in the dirt (this is a pun) to fight a price war. We made **quality** our slogan, and we rode it into victory over all the competition.

POLICY ON PRICES

Price wars are hopeless. You can never win a price war. All you can do is shoot yourself in the foot if you engage in a price war.

This is especially true of the young, independent producer, but it applies to everybody at all times.

Let's start with an *honest price*. I call it an honest price if it carries a proper advertising allowance, a research allowance and incentives for sales momentum, plus whatever is prevailing in the retail stores. That's about as honest as you can get.

Any fatcat can compete with your price by pushing "Lost Leaders", content to suffer losses until *you* go out of business. He can undercut you on price if he bypasses quality. If you in turn lower quality, you're wrong.

It's a nerve-wracking situation— I've been through it, and thank the Lord I was able to hold my own. Somebody can always do it cheaper. That is easy enough. But to do it more cheaply without cheapening the quality—that's a tough thing to do. *I say* you can't give in to the cheaper price; you might have to lose some customers. Hold your own and keep reminding them that they are paying a price in quality for the advantage they find in pricing.

We always geared our production, as well as promotional strategy, to the people who liked their cats. Our basic platform was LOVE. I told them *"Edward Lowe loves your cat."* My sales showed they believed me. Cat lovers are not about to supply their cats with an inferior product which won't satisfy the cat's needs, or may possibly injure the cat. Gerber's could probably get by with using second-rate vegetables in their baby food. They don't do this because parents won't take second-best for their baby. You take care of the baby, and you take care of the cat. *There is love at stake*. It's hard to put a price tag on love, but the Kitty Litter story tells you that love, backed up by quality and the sincere effects of thorough research, will triumph over the discounted "bargains".

THE PERSONAL APPROACH

Somebody said that *"the institution is the lengthened shadow of the man."* I'm not sure who "General" Motors is. I can't even say if there is a "Colonel" or a "Lieutenant" Motors. There *was* a "Henry Ford" and I know there is a "Mary Kay". I happen to believe that it makes a big difference if a human being—a single personality—is behind the goods and the service.

My concept of the entrepreneurial system is that it is *not* compatible with remote control or absentee ownership. The entrepreneur operates a hands-on administration of his company. When his name and his reputation are on the line with the integrity of his offering, the public *knows* who to blame and who to trust, or not trust.

I had to overcome resistance in my advertising agencies (who were spending millions of my dollars) before I could put my own picture on the package, and appear in my own TV commercials. They thought it was "client vanity." My "vanity" is such that I'd rather not be seen at all. But with my conviction that the public should know who was behind Kitty Litter, my picture went on the pack and I went on the commercials, and guess what? *Sales went up.*

Edward Lowe Loves Your Cat. (The cat couldn't read but the owner did and believed me.)

My personalized presentation was started with the brokers. They all knew who I was; they all knew I would live up to my word. The people that work for you and the people that buy your product should be on a first name basis. When my payroll exceeded seven hundred I couldn't possibly know each of them by name, but I always called them Chief or something, so they knew I recognized them. And I'll tell you something: most of them thought they knew me. Well, they *did* know me because I came into their workplaces, mixed with them and talked to them. Showed that I cared by paying good wages and keeping a clean shop.

But you know you have to do almost the same thing with your customers. I've got files of fan letters, literally thousands of them. It's all a matter of people talking to a real person, not a dehumanized corporate image.

You can't establish a personal connection with a cat. A cat "Frankly, my dear..." doesn't give a dang. But I let the people that own the cat know Edward Lowe does love your cat. That was my theme and as I said it worked.

QUALITY CONTROL OUTSIDE

What a lot of start-up enterprisers don't yet comprehend is that quality control goes deeper than the product you manufacture under your own roof. So many of the materials you buy from outside suppliers play a critical part in preserving your quality.

For example, what if the bags you buy to put your product in are defective or underqualified? They may break as your customer carries the bag upstairs. Take a little thing (or one that looks trivial)—the string that sews the bag. Your product can be deteriorated in shipment. You can only entrust it to quality trucking firms that know how to transport your goods.

There are countless points of quality vulnerability, even hazardous points. You have got to be on the alert, keeping track of your material all the way from drawing-board to customer consumption. I'll tell you one thing more, something that wasn't in style a few years ago—if your competition is guilty of a quality defect, blow the whistle! Let the public know.

PACKAGING

Whatever product you may come up with, it will go to the customer in some form of a package. It may be a crate and barrel or a shopping bag, but your product—meaning your name, your reputation and your chances for a repeat purchase all end up in that package.

All of this means that your packaging is a vital form of advertising—whether it serves as a billboard on a shelf or a portable device to get the product to the customer's home. Color is a big thing. Never forget the power of colors. As you walk down the aisle, you're tied to the magnetic pull of color. Red, white and blue are powerful, for obvious reasons. Yellow is a strong draw.

I noticed one product package the other day that changed colors to a washed-out blue and forgot the yellow and black. Black is sort of a skeleton on which the vivid colors can stand. There are trends, of course, but if a change is called for, never go to a weaker color.

Every package is a miniature billboard, carrying your message everywhere it goes. It's surprising how many people in business don't realize that. Next time you're in a supermarket, take a look at the "Out of Stock" items now on sale at discounts. Look at them, and you'll see they are dullards in color and package design.

I mention these often overlooked items to show the coming generation the endless variety of details that the entrepreneur has to confront. This is not the place to discuss other obligations such as buying land, negotiating deals and contracts, setting up manufacturing plants and inventing machinery for their improvement, or plotting the distribution of your product from coast to coast.

The entrepreneur wears all of these hats. It's no role for a sleepyhead to play. It takes energy, initiative and a lot of guts.

I did it. This book and its several sections will give you a good insight into *how* I did it. My dearest wish is that it will help you in your business career.

Ponder that statement for a while.

HIGHLIGHTS OF A SPEECH BY EDWARD LOWE AT GREEN BAY, WISCONSIN

(EXCERPTS)

AN OATH TO TAKE

I like to ask my audiences this—how many of you were Boy Scouts or Girl Scouts? Will you stand up please? Give me the hand signal and repeat with me: On my honor I will do my best to do my duty to God and my country, and obey Scout laws and help other people at all times, keep myself physically strong, mentally awake and morally straight. I will be obedient, cheerful, thrifty, brave, clean, reverent, trust-worthy, loyal, helpful, friendly, cour-teous and kind.

I tell you I'd feel a heck of a lot better if the President of the United States took that pledge, wouldn't you?

EVERYTHING I KNOW

This illustrates the price of stand-ing up in front of a crowd. About fif-teen years ago I was talking to some Junior Achievers, trying to cultivate their ability as young entrepreneurs to start their own businesses. After one session I got a letter from a young fellow by the name of Tommy Weersma, from Warren Pennsylvania. It said, "Dear Mr. Lowe (spelled d-e-e-r) I met you yesterday. You invented Kitty Litter and made a lot of money. That's what I'd like to do. Enclosed is one dollar. **Write back and tell me everything you know.**"

I kept that letter, because some-times you think you know every-thing, but you hardly ever do.

WHAT SMALL BUSINESS IS

I don't happen to believe that there is such a thing as a "small" business. Not in the sense that it is unimportant or trivial.

To every person here, whether they are a loner or have only two or more employees, their enterprise is a BIG business. The problem is—do you know what the government classifies as "a small business"? Let me tell you: "small business" in the eyes of the government, is any outfit with fewer than *five hundred employees!* Can you imagine that? Is there anyone here who hires five hundred people? The government is looking down the wrong end of the funnel. To me a small business is a company that is run by an individual or a family in a range of 45 or 50 employees. That seems to me to be a nice *big* small business.

KNOWING HOW TO DO IT

As far as I'm concerned, one of the big problems with small busi-ness is that *you don't know how to run your business.*

Don't take this wrong—the rea-son you don't know how to run the business, doggone it, is that *you don't have time to learn HOW to run your business.* Why? Because you're too busy with all the paper work and the busy-busy things the government insists you have to do.

You are overwhelmed with rules and regulations and time-consuming red tape problems that are really not a part of basic business operation.

EDUCATING OURSELVES

There is no doubt we have to develop some form of meaningful education for our business managers. We can't expect to go to academia and get good help from the professors there. They are teaching from *books* that were written by other teachers who had read some books. The students who get out of college today only know book learning—*if* they know how to read and write. Real life in the small business world isn't like that. When you run into a problem in your machine shop, when something goes wrong, you don't go to any book to look it up. You roll up your sleeves, put on your gloves and go in and solve the problem.

You're not going to be able to do that unless we build some workable form of communication. That's what we're doing at the Edward Lowe Foundation.

WHAT COMES NEXT?

Yes, our Foundation is engaged in developing and promoting a program we can bring young people into, middle-aged people, and some of us older guys—to teach us what's wrong with our business methods and how to improve them.

You may not know what's holding your business back, but 90% of the time it's the president or the owner. If he's a single owner—*he's the problem*. I'll tell you why: the entrepreneur has very special problems. For one thing, he usually talks to no one. He thinks he knows it all. He's forward and he's uncouth. I know, *because I am one*. We are an isolated bunch of creative people who've been cut off from the vital pool of information. *Our Foundation is making available a network system which provides access to that information.*

LOOKING FAR AHEAD

The important motive is to carry on forever. That's the goal. This applies to the name of Edward Lowe, the Academy, and our Mission. We are doing this through the complex form of a Foundation, The Edward Lowe Foundation. The monumental structure of such a Foundation as determined by the federal IRS causes great concern and sometimes calls for decisions that boggle my mind. But it must be done, and so the fortune amassed over the last 45 years will be directed to the Foundation. The statement I find intriguing is "*That He who gives while he lives knows where it goes*". It supports the decision that Darlene and I have followed, giving all of our efforts to the Edward Lowe Foundation and its mission to revive the entrepreneur who is an endangered species.

The Edward Lowe Free Enterprise Theatre Presents:

HATS!

A VIDEO SKIT

(The skit opens with a long pan shot of a row of hats hanging on a rack with a series of pegs, showing hats ranging from cowboy hat to derby, etc. Ed Lowe walks on camera and picks up the cowboy hat.)

And hats off to you, pardners! Do you remember that in the old cowboy movies you could always tell the good guys from the bad guys by the hats they were wearing?

The heroes were easy to spot because they were wearing the white hats. Hoot Gibson, Tom Mix, Colonel Tim McCoy—they'd never be seen without a white hat.

(Points to row of hats)

My main message to wouldbe entrepreneurs is that there is no *one* hat for you to wear. If you are looking for your one favorite hat style, you're out of luck.

(Sweeps hand along the hat line-up)

You'd better be prepared to wear all these hats! This is because the entrepreneur has got to be a jack of all trades in order to be master of the company he or she calls their own.

Our main interest, really our *only* interest, is in the entrepreneur. I kinda consider myself the haberdasher for the entrepreneur. I'm here to tell the entrepreneur what to wear.

(He picks up graduate's cap and holds it before camera.)

We know the entrepreneur is a thinker, a dreamer, a scholar and an innovator. He not only works like a horse, but he ponders away, thinking up ways and means to better his product and better his sales.

He or she is a dreamer who thinks and a thinker who dreams. A planner and a doer. Whenever you think of an entrepreneur or wonder if you are one yourself, remember that your whole career starts with an idea, or a set of ideas—ideas you *yourself* nurse and bring into action.

(He puts cap back on rack and selects the derby.)

Very soon in his career he has to learn what cash flow is and how to balance his books. He has to count on his profit and loss situation, and also to get skilled help in his accounting.

The entrepreneur may feel a little bashful about looking and acting like a businessman with a derby like this, but you'd better get used to it. The nuts and bolts of your enterprise are the dollars and cents in your P. and L. which is your scoreboard.

(He replaces derby and selects mechanic's cap)

You know, we need a new color description for the entrepreneur. We've got the *"white* collar" executive and the *"blue* collar" worker and that's not enough for our species. I guess we represent the *red, white and blue collar* because we have grease on our hands, too.

The entrepreneur doesn't have time to look in the yellow pages every time his company runs into a snag. He is the builder of the enterprise: he knows how it works and if it doesn't work he knows how to fix it.

He has to be master of his mechanical operation, the nuts and bolts of whatever his company does. If there's a breakdown he has to know how to fix it, or at least give it a good try.

(Replaces mechanic's hat and selects a military captain's cap)

The entrepreneur, man or woman, is a pace-setter, a Ramrod who gets things done. The operation is a hands-on business. There's no long distance, remote control relationship. It's highly individualized, highly personalized. And if the endangered species is to survive, the leadership principle will be personified.

From the word "Go" he has to be a leader able to organize his workforce as a team, able to inspire it and motivate it. And he stays in front of the parade, no armchair captain is he!

(Ed selects Driver's Cap with goggles)

None of this means that the entrepreneur can be a stay-at-home stick-in-the-mud, remaining isolated from the marketplace. He or she must be on the "go", learning the field, making friends and getting the product, whatever it is, on the shelves where it belongs.

This entrepreneur has to get his product to market. He has to put the rubber on the road, out finding his customers, introducing his goods and making friends.

(Now Ed selects a straw hat)

Once he meets and knows his customers in the marketplace, the entrepreneur has to know how to *sell* his goods. This means that he not only believes in his product, but he has the ability to convince his prospects that they should believe in it, too. This calls for *sincerity*. Selling is not a confidence game. No matter how many phonies are doing it.

Selling a good product is a matter of making friends. Friendship is built by telling the truth about what you are selling. And backing up your promises.

(Ed carefully pulls down a steel helmet. Studies it somberly.)

I know very well what this signifies. I've been through it. Let's say you come out with a brand-new product and it has implications you can't even imagine. All of a sudden, some of the biggest corporations in the industry aim their guns on you. Let me tell you, it can get a little scary...

Don't laugh, it's a real war out there, and he has to be ready to face the heavy fire of his competition. They're going to try to gun him down from inside and outside, be ready!

(He selects an artist's beret)

Your job is not only to defend your existence. The entrepreneur has to be *continually* creative, all along the highway to success. You can hire experts and agencies, but mainly it is the entrepreneur's job to frame his appeal to his market. He has to become a master of his own story and learn the art of advertising it. He has to be a showman, keeping his audience entertained while he has the chance to sell his wares. When he's out in front, he's always on stage...

(He reaches for the Uncle Sam's striped hat)

There are a lot more hats, but I hope I've proven to you that the entrepreneur has to wear many, *many* hats. It is definitely not a one-hat job, as you can see.

This hat is always in his rack. He's never ashamed to wear this hat.

The entrepreneur is always a good citizen. He's a loyal American and loves his country. At the same time he doesn't let the bureaucrats ride roughshod over him. In the true American spirit, he guards his rights and defends himself against oppression.

The forefathers who set this country up are sort of depending on us right now to hold on to basic liberties and keep the American way flourishing.

As you see, the entrepreneur wears a whale of a lot of hats! and with very good reason... for lots of reasons—we've become handicapped by overspecialization and too tight job-classification. You know very well what I mean. A pipefitter is not allowed to hammer a nail. The carpenter can't replace a light bulb. The electrician can't—well, you know the story. Job jurisdiction has kept each member on the team confined to his or her place on the assembly line. This ends up where maintenance people don't have any notion of what happens in production. Workers in make-ready are totally ignorant of what happens in final assembly. This kind of isolation is something the entrepreneurial system just can't tolerate.

"Free enterprise" is a two-word program. It's the entrepreneur that brings *both* words to life. "Hard work" and "imagination" give us "enterprise", which isn't quite enough. The entrepreneur's sense of independence and pursuit of excellence keeps it "free."

(Close-up to Ed as he selects the white cowboy hat shown at the opening.)

America is in need of some heroes right now. You, too, can be a hero and help strengthen our free enterprise business economy.

So let's get this show on the road!

And hold onto your hats, my fellow entrepreneurs, because we're traveling in the fast lane!

(Fade Out)

LETTER TO AUSTIN

I'll tell you somethin'—I happen to be dog-gonned proud of my grandson Eddie, who is your Grandpa, Austin. I always managed to pay my way and keep my family in a secure way, but your Grandpa Lowe has really made a name for himself! And he's developed a pretty impressive business while doing it. Good for him, I say!

What I want to tell you now has to do with wealthy men. Without taking one smidgin of respect away from Grandpa Lowe, I don't want you to be over-impressed by "Big Money", all by itself. There's a lot of different ways to judge big fortunes, and I'm here to give you a basic standard to go by.

Big Money gives its holders a lot of leeway. They can always brag about how they used their wealth to help this or that and do some good by it. Sure, that's one standard, Austin, and it's not a bad one. But there is a better rule than that.

You've gotta look deep to find it, but there's the question: <u>Who did they hurt in acquiring their wealth?</u> That's a serious question. You'd be surprised how the "lust for gold" has injured a lot of folks on the wayside while the Money Moguls were accumulating the stuff. Which is one reason I'm so very proud of your Grandpa, boy...

Check him out, and you'll find that he didn't hurt anybody at all-not a single person, while making a name for himself and a healthy business while he was at it.

This can be proven out: he always was fair to his employees, his neighbors, his competition. He never did anything that damaged the environment, and his products always helped whatever they were intended to help.

O yes, the Edward Lowe Foundation does a heap of good, but what I want you to know is that while Eddie was making that Foundation possible he didn't hurt a single soul!

Love ya,

Grandpa Huber

SECTION TWO

UNDERSTANDING ECONOMICS

Dear Reader,

If you are going to play the game (and I hope you intend to) then you had better understand what the game is all about. And if you are an entrepreneur or want to be, then this understanding is **very important** for your welfare.

Edward Lowe

ECONOMICS

PLAIN TALK

By Edward Lowe

What is this thing we call *"The Economy"*?

What is this system we call *"Economics"*?

Thomas Carlyle (1795-1881) called "economics" the *dismal science.*

It's pretty doggonned dismal, the way it's going.

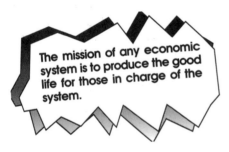

The mission of any economic system is to produce the good life for those in charge of the system.

Some consider it *"The art of managing the resources of a people and its government."*

If it's an art, where are the artists?

Another view calls it *"the theoretical science of the laws of production and distribution."*

Production is a practical matter; I don't think the "science" should be very "theoretical."

ECONOMICS IS A HUMAN INSTITUTION

It is often influenced by Mother Nature, by flood and drought, frost and volcanic eruption—*but...*

...It is a system created by mankind for human benefits, so that people can create the wealth it takes so they may live together in relative comfort...

The American Free Enterprise System is the first in the history of the world with the potential to produce a comfortable living for all who are free, able and willing to work for it...

Unless it is interfered with!

TAKE YOUR PICK!

Is it an "art"?
"a theoretical science"?
"a body of knowledge"?
or just "a term" we use?

I decided to pick the thing apart and see what it's made of. Bear with me while I separate the main parts as I see them, and maybe we can figure what it's all about...

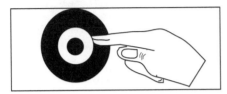

To begin with, I know what a "market" is. When I was a boy we'd go to the market early in the morning. The farmers had all brought their goods in and had their wagons laid out to display their wares. Everybody could walk around and buy whatever they needed and liked. "Going to market" was a big deal.

So I know what a *market is*...

This is what we call *"The Market"*

A place where buying and selling is going on.

It includes all the people who have needs and desires and the purchasing power ($$$) to buy the goods and services which are being offered for sale to satisfy their needs and desires.

If you're going into the market, you'd better have some idea of what's happening there...

Whatever the category, there is usually a place where that trade is concentrated, whether it be farm produce, stocks and bonds, oil, futures, etc.

All the producing members of the general market form a "hub" in their particular marketplace to produce all the things the market has an appetite (demand) for...

Finding *your* marketplace, the best target for *your* offering, is one of your first requirements.

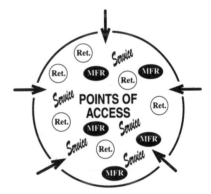

WHAT IS A "FREE MARKET"?

A free market allows competition between all voluntary producers and vendors of goods and services. It allows consumers to buy from whichever sources they prefer to buy from—without coercion or excessive regulation.

When this is "capped" under Soviet statism the free enterprise fire goes out.

The entrepreneur cannot prosper in a stifled (capped) economy!

To keep the economy free, keep the lid off!

**Buy and sell as we choose
or our freedom we lose
Let's do as our founders did
when they knocked off the
Empire's lid**

—*E. Lowe*

I am beginning to see what's behind the word "Economics"...

"Eco" basically means your **environment** (as used in "ecology"). "-nomics" generally stands for "supply".

Put them together and "economics" is **"How your environment nourishes itself."**

Once I got this far, I was getting the hang of it. I was beginning to see "economics" as more than a lifeless abstraction.

I was beginning to see it as an **organism**—an organized body of mutual and dependent parts constituted **to share a common life.**

I knew that "biology" is the study of natural life. What I was doing was trying to study a **living** economy. **Stay with me...**

A NOTICE TO ALL ENTREPRENEURS

A free economy is a living economy. A living economy is an interchange of manufactured products, skilled crafts & services uninhibited by excessive regulations. All bought and sold and/or bartered by customers who are free to buy or not buy as their judgement or budget permits. When this freedom is diminished, the economy loses its life and vitality.

LETTER TO AUSTIN

Hi! I'd like to put a bug in your ear about this thing they call "environment". You're hearing a lot about it, I know. In my day, and in your Grandpa's day, we didn't call it that. We just referred to "<u>the world around us</u>"—something like that. But today it's different. "Environment" is quite a buzz word and I know darn well that you're going to be hit over the head with it.

You're going to be told that environment is mostly a matter of clean air, whales, spotted owls and getting rid of hazardous waste. Of course, those are all big things, buddy, but when you consider environment as a <u>whole</u>, they are really not the biggest things.

The greatest single factor when you're talking about a <u>people-environment</u> is the PEOPLE in it. I don't want you to lose sight of that. Sometimes we get so darned complicated we pass over the simple but basic things.

Now the greatest single issue concerning people is: how do they make a living? Keeping people alive is a very big deal or the environment can go jump in the lake. Before people can live, either well or badly, they have to make a living. Their environment had best deal with that question first and foremost.

Once people are making a comfortable living—enough to keep a home and family together—then they can look after the issues in the natural world which might harm the way they live (the air and water and hazardous waste.)

After all that is handled, we can look after the spotted owl.

Loveya
Grandpa Huber

SO I PONDERED...

WHAT MAKES A SYSTEM LIKE THIS COME TO LIFE?

I can see it's a network of interchanges involving a whole bunch of people... but what is it that makes that network a living system?

I WONDERED....

Then it came to me...

The Growth Dynamic is the **key**

characteristic of all living things (human, animal or vegetable)

If there is no dynamism of growth, then there is no longer life

GROWTH!

WHERE DOES IT COME FROM?

THE ALGEBRAIC FORMULA FOR THE ENTREPRENEUR

TO YOU IT'S UNIQUE
YOU KNOW ME.
TO ME IT'S UNIQUE
I KNOW YOU.

SO Y + M = M + Y

Y2 + M2 = YM4

SO

TO **BE** UNIQUE AND
KNOW UNIQUE
TO **KNOW** UNIQUE AND
BE UNIQUE
FORMULATES TO
BU + KU = BU + KU
BU2 + KU2 = BKU4

THE $\dfrac{YM^4}{BKU^4}$ = YMB^{2}K^{2}U^1 =

KNOW^2 YOU^{1+}
KNOW^2 ME =
B^2 KNOWLEDGEABLE +
K^2 KNOWLEDGEABLE =
$\dfrac{YM}{BKU}$ = YMBKU

THE ENTREPRENEUR

The Edward Lowe Free Enterprise Theatre Presents:

"The Miracle Of Smallness"

A VIDEO SKIT

(Edward Lowe is seated at a laboratory table peering into the lens of an impressive microscope. On the wall behind him hangs a chart—the kind often seen in a doctor's office, showing circulatory system, muscles, nerves etc... Also on the table are a thick dictionary, a folded newspaper and a small model airplane.)

E.L. *(Thinking out loud)* Now isn't that strange! I've got a drop of water under the microscope—just a drop of ordinary tap water—and would you believe it? There's a **whole world** going on inside that tiny drop of water. It's like an aquarium! Strange things swimming around in there! It's hard to believe...!

(Turns to look at chart)

When you think about how complicated the human body is, and all the activity going on inside **it**, you know there's a lot of water over the dam! I wonder what we've learned from being able to see all these invisible worlds?

(Leafs through dictionary)

It says here that the cell is "**the ultimate element in organic structures.**" Wow! If you think about it, the discovery of the cell as the smallest building block in the body was a tremendous discovery—a more important event than walking on the moon!

(He talks directly to camera)

You know, it's kind of crazy the way we worship **bigness** when the miracle of smallness is right here under our eyes. All the competition today is to see what can be bigger than the biggest. If it's big, OK—but is it bigger than anything there ever was before?

(Looks again into microscope lens)

You get so big and what happens? Ask the dinosaur—if you can find one. The huge dinosaur disappeared, but the tiny red ants are running around everywhere.

(He walks around in front of table)

If basketball players get any bigger, we'll have to build new gymnasiums. But, did you ever notice—candy bars are getting smaller and smaller— **while the price keeps going up?**

(Returns to microscope lens)

Bigness gets to be a joke after a while—especially after you know that *smallness* is the heart of the matter. (Picks up model airplane.) Look at airplanes, and how they have grown. Did you know that the little baby the Wright Brothers made could have flown *inside* a 747? Remember Howard Hughes? Well, Howard Hughes built the biggest plane ever to fly. He made it out of plywood and he called it *"The Spruce Goose."* He flew it about 20 feet off the ground for about 200 yards or so, just to prove it would fly. Then he put it away in storage. It was another dinosaur, I guess.

(Pats the microscope)

In my opinion, this baby here is more important than the telescope. I know that most folks are fascinated with wondering if there is life on Mars, when they haven't got the foggiest idea of how much life there is in the glass of water they are drinking. I'm here to tell you that *smallness* is the name of the game...

(Picks up newspaper, scans it)

Here it is—look here—all over the world they are worried about nuclear arsenals. That's the atom bomb. They make the *biggest* explosion, but the atom had to be discovered before they could split it up and make it go *"Boom".* Do you know what that little old atom was called. It was *"the ultimate particle of matter."* Just like the cell was *"the ultimate element."* It's all a miracle of smallness, isn't it? How small do you want to go?

(Reading more stories in paper)

There's a story bigger than bombs. Do you know what it is? It's the *computer.* Hey, they keep getting *smaller and smaller,* don't they? The first one IBM built 45 years ago would fill a couple of rooms. Now they are *lap-sized.* Next thing you know, they'll fit into your pocket.

That's what I call *"the miracle of smallness".* We focused smaller and smaller—from the transistor down to the micro-chip. And in those tiny bits we are able to program highly complicated routines of command performance.

(Turns page of newspaper)

In the meantime, the news is crowded with stories about *bigness.* Big Business is laying off thousands of workers. Big Banking is having trouble with the big interest rate. Big Government is struggling with a National Debt that is bigger than it is. How do we get loose from this cult of bigness and get down to the brass tacks of *ultimate reality* in our daily affairs?

(Seats himself)

That's why I looked at our economic system. I studied it as close as you can study a drop of water. I freed my mind from all the abstractions about how *immense* our economy was, and how *big* its problems were. I was looking for the *ultimate element* in our economy. I looked everywhere.

(Turns head in every direction)

I looked at theories. I looked at flow charts. I looked at socio-economic classes. I looked at industrial statistics. I was trying to find the basic building block...

(To camera)

I finally found it. It all narrowed down to an *individual* human being. It wasn't any great overpowering dinosaur. *It was you!* The sparkplug that jumpstarts the whole motor. The cell that triggers the operation...

(Points finger at camera). *It's you! (He salutes)*

Hail entrepreneur!

Economics is a man-made system and the basic cell of that system is man himself. It's no mystery. It's no abstraction. It's a natural development, operating as a living natural organism.

God Bless America!

Why does a snake shed its skin?

THE LAWS OF LIFE

To understand "Economics" as a living organic system we need to investigate.

1. All living beings are formed of "cells".

2. The basic unit of the living body is "the cell".

3. Each cell is a tiny packet of life.

4. All cells grow through *cell division.*

5. If cell growth stops, life stops.

HOW DOES THE CELL GROW?

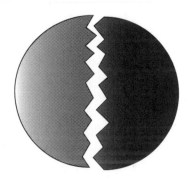

It divides itself.

• it separates itself into two parts.

• It becomes more than it was.

• It creates another life outside itself.

• That's how it grows

(But *only* if it has been able to draw energy from its environment in order to be vitalized.)

And only if no outside force has interfered with its natural process!

(Which can be cancerous.)

WHY DOES THE CELL DIVIDE?

(Just to keep itself busy?)

A snake sheds its skin every season but *not* because it wants to be in step with the Spring fashions.

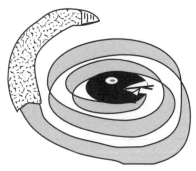

A snake sheds its skin because the old skin is *too tight.* It *must* get free of the straitjacket in order to live.

The cell has no choice either!

It *must* divide because its energy supply is too much for *one* cell.

Growth is not an option.

It is a vital neccesity.

All living things share basic life processes—so we must find out...

What is the Ecomomic Cell?

The Entrepreneur has a built-in talent for creating new answers for old problems

New WAYS OF DOING THINGS New METHODS, New PRODUCTS BETTER SOLUTIONS FOR Better Living

That's why the Entrepreneur is the Growth Cell of the living economy.

He (or She) can't help it...

The Entrepreneur *must* be allowed to foster economic growth.

America's economic growth depends on the Entrepreneur.

The Entrepreneur requires:

- *Energy*
- *Encouragement*
- *Opportunity*

Snuff out entrepreneurism and all of small, independently-owned business will suffer.

The collectivised states of the world show us how initiative, imagination and enthusiasm disappear when the individual entrepreneur is wiped out.

Crush the Entrepreneur and Economic Growth stops.

America's greatness has grown because *Free Enterprise* encouraged the Entrepreneur.

(And the Entrepreneur was the motor force for the growth of Free Enterprise.)

America's greatness is threatened today by the increased frustrations of the entrepreneur and the increasing strangulation of small, independent businesses.

S.O.S.

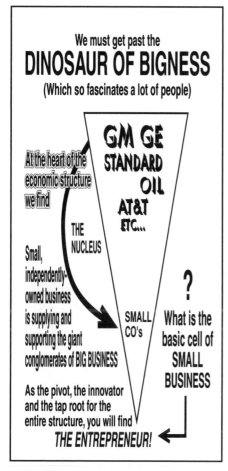

We must get past the

DINOSAUR OF BIGNESS

(Which so fascinates a lot of people)

At the heart of the economic structure we find

GM GE STANDARD OIL AT&T ETC...

THE NUCLEUS

Small, independently-owned business is supplying and supporting the giant conglomerates of BIG BUSINESS

SMALL CO's

? What is the basic cell of SMALL BUSINESS

As the pivot, the innovator and the tap root for the entire structure, you will find

THE ENTREPRENEUR!

WHAT IS IT?

What distinguishes this element we call the *most important* in the small business universe?

It is the Entrepreneur who

•takes the risk of departing from the established track.

• dares experiment with inventions and innovations.

* will take off on independent projects all alone

• will pursue a precedent-break-ing idea until it sinks or swims

• cannot resist the opportunity to blaze new trails.

HAIL ENTREPRENEUR!

YES!

The individual entrepeneur is the basic creative cell of the economic network

The entrepreneur is the "Growth Cell"

The entrepreneur has the built-in compulsion to "cell-divide" the present from the future, creatively breaking ground for progess.

(Producing such things as the Model T, corn flakes, the transistor and Kitty Litter)

You don't teach a Beagle to hunt Rabbits.

It has its own inbred drive to do so.

It *wants* to hunt rabbits

It *likes* to hunt rabbits

It *needs* to hunt rabbits

So it is with *The Entrepreneur!*

His creative energy is where small business begins

Why is the entrepreneur so important to Edward Lowe?

Because his creative energy supports the entire free enterprise economy.

Because its future and his productivity are threatened today.

The Entrepreneur with his creative energy is where small business begins.

"If the entrepreneur is crushed, the whole structure of small business will deteriorate."

Small business creates the majority of new jobs, generates most new inventions, supplies big business vital material.

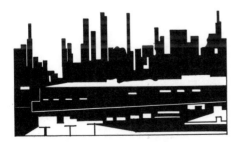

"If small business deteriorates because the entrepreneur has been smothered, then the superstructure of Big Business will sooner or later fall apart."

Today the Entrepreneur is harassed by the brick walls of...

"The threat to the Entrepreneur is a threat to the American dynamic. At the very moment when the world (especially in Europe and Asia) is desperately in need of free market leadership in the American tradition....!."

Wake up, Congress!

What made the U.S. the world's richest nation with the highest living standards of any people on the face of the earth?

"It was the creative energy of the entrepreneur flourishing under a Constitutional freedom which allowed us to prosper."

WHAT IS HAPPENING NOW

In the United States entrepreneurship is discouraged, is being penalized and ignored by our national leadership...
President & staff and Congress.

In Europe, the old Soviet Union and in China, they are yearning to free enterprise leadership from slave labor.

WHAT SHOULD HAPPEN

Our economy led the world once. Based on the free entrepreneur our free economy can do it again!

Let us give it a chance!

TO THE ENTREPRENEUR

Oh fame, to you who lack the fame,
Whose wanton acts won't gather gain.
To those who dander, sally forth
Expecting small or little growth.

Small rewards, the trapper gored.
Trader, warrior, wielding sword.
His fame not noticed, spoken nare;
His name forgotten, grizzly bear.

But to his heart's frozen throb,
He did his most, to him his job.
His heart's hot blood did pour
For satisfaction, not much more.

A PERSONAL WORD FROM THE AUTHOR

I want to remind you of something which I think you need reminding of. As you read this book you are running into this term "entrepreneur" over and over, and I know this is not a new word for you. In fact it has become a "buzz word" and is very popular these days, standing for just about anything or anybody.

As I use the term and as I have defined it, you will be understanding the historical meaning of "entrepreneur", as nobody that I know of has so far presented.

I want you to see this person "the entrepreneur" as an old breed in the American tradition—but as of today, very much in danger, of being crushed by Big Brother.

THE MODERN MOUNTAIN MEN

Where do they roam,
When do they storm,
To the peak of a
Challenging mountain?

Where is their valley
Of despair that they found
That they flounder through, that
They wander through?

Where is their strength
That holds back tears
When they hear the jeers
of those behind who
Were not their peers?

Who laugh to the beat of
An off-tune band
That "Hail to the Entrepreneur"
Can't stand.

—Edward Lowe

This is a Tree, This is not all the tree.

(It is not even the most important part of the tree.)

Like every living thing the tree is made up of *cells*. Cells form the leaves, the branches and the trunk. Of course, they also form the root structure.

The roots of the tree underground are the *foundation* of the tree. The tree lives and grows through the strength of the roots.

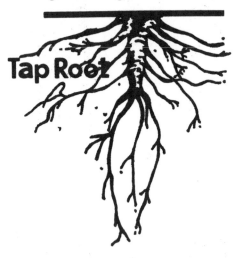

One root is the vital part of the root structure.

That is the Tap Root.

The tap root is the root which searches for nourishment in the soil and leads all the other root stems to it.

Kill the tap root and you kill the tree!

In the economic body the entrepreneur leads the way through initiative, innovation and experimentation. The entrepreneur searches for new answers to old problems, daring to find fertile soil for the roots of the general welfare.

The tap root is the entrepreneur.

LETTER TO AUSTIN

Hello there! Buddy, if you decide, as I hope someday you will decide, to follow in your Grandpa Lowe's footsteps, there's a big decision you'll have to make, And I want to help you, if you decide to go that way.

The biggest decision the wouldbe entrepreneur has to make is to *"go your own way."* Independence is the big deal. That's the biggest step you'll have to take.

It means, first of all, trusting yourself. You have to be brave enough to trust your own "gut feelings." You have to dare to go against the grain, cultivating your personal point of view, based on knowledge you have gotten hold of. Then you've got to generate enough energy to get your program off the ground and build some benefits with it.

But, Austin, there's a stiff price you pay for that kind of independence...

You tend to be isolated. It's called *"loneliness"*. You tend to be all alone. You get so sensitive (even jealous) about protecting your independence that you lose contact with valuable sources of help. You tend to cut yourself off from important contacts.

Grandpa Lowe can tell you how to avoid this. What you have to do, buddy, is to keep your eye open for reinforcements all along the way. Don't give up the search for minds and hands that can serve your cause.

Heck yes, You'll run into a lot of counterfeits, and your Grandpa Lowe can give you chapter and verse on that danger. But don't let yourself become a "loner" cast in iron. Keep your eyes and your heart open for true friends and helpful allies.

Loveya

Grandpa Huber

Explain relativity in 25 words or less...

Reprinted from Edward Lowe's MAIN STREET JOURNAL

EDWARD LOWE'S CELL SYSTEM

In Theory and in Practice

"What is the *Cell System*" I asked Ed Lowe. "Simply put."

"Would you ask Einstein to explain relativity to you in 25 words or less?" he responded.

"I might."

"Well, he wouldn't have answered you," Ed told me. "But I will. Think of a box."

"A box?" "Yes, a box. Isn't that simple enough? Like a casket, where you put a dead body in it and then nail a lid on the top."

I thought of such a box. It was all my own fault. The Edward Lowe application for the prestigious Rolex Award is based on Ed's inventive formulation called "The Cell System". It carries a number of scholarly papers and a full file of case histories and support material. I wanted a neat little definition I could print in this column.

"Am I going too fast for you?" Ed asked.

"Oh no. I'm taking notes," I told him.

"Now think of another box—a flower box."

"Another box?"

"Yep. With good, rich garden soil, well-ventilated, and open to sunlight and regular watering. Got it?"

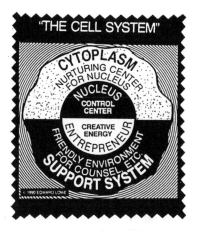

"Got it." I said "And that's the Cell System, is it—*a casket and a flower box?"*

"Nope. they are just for openers. You know what I think of the entrepreneur, I assume?"

I knew very well because Ed Lowe has made a career out of redefining the entrepreneur as the vital energy source of a dynamic economy. "Yessir. You're sorta fond of the entrepreneur."

"Right on! So let's call the entrepreneurial dynamic *'the spirit of enterprise'*. That 'spirit of enterprise' is germinal. It is the growth source—the *seed.* Like a seed it has to be planted. Are you with me?"

"Almost," I said. "What about those boxes?"

"The box with the lid, the one that looks like a casket, is the conventional corporate structure of today. It's a pyramid with topdown directives and no room for an entrepreneur to grow. You can't put him in a box like that without suffocating his initiative, his incentive for innovation and his natural yearning to blaze new trails." Ed was very serious about this.

"So where is the Cell System of yours?'"

"I am glad you asked," he said. "What the Cell System does is to turn a casket into a fertile flower box where the spirit of enterprise can grow. That spirit just plain withers away in the bureaucratic atmosphere of the typical business organization. The Cell System cushions the entrepreneurial nucleus with helpful accessories, usable know-how, like-minded counselors and the ways and means to grow."

"You're telling me that economics is a natural, organic thing and not some cut-and-dried theoretical system?'"

"I sure am. What is economics? *It's human beings in commerce with one another.* Put it in a casket and the will to grow chokes up and dies."

I had one more question of Ed. "Just how did you discover this Cell System theory of yours?'

"I stayed out of the closed box," he told me.

"You never went Wall Street, did you?"

"Nope," he smiled. "I'm 100% Main Street, from the ground up."

If anything is alive, it's growing. When growth stops, life stops. Ed

knew this was as true of a business organization as it was of human beings. The only difference was that in the business world, cadavers kept hanging around, cluttering up the economic landscape.

Any kind of growth makes a difference. There is no growth without exploring the unknown. Stay-at-homes, assets-managers and bottom liners may keep the home fires burning, but it is the scouts who leave home and brave the wilderness who create the change. They are the entrepreneurs—the *engineers of growth.*

Until he was successful, Ed Lowe didn't know the word "entrepreneur." It is a term that has been vulgarized by over-use and misunderstanding. Many think it means a combination of a snake oil salesmen and a riverboat gambler. Not even slightly true.

Ed knew he was an inventor (he holds some 17 patents). He knew he was an innovator (of Kitty Litter® and other break-through products). He knew he had to assess and acquire industrial real estate, build plants, and manage the productivity of those plants. He knew he had to hire and administer a pretty hefty payroll of 700 employees. He had to design packaging and advertising materials and then "put the rubber on the road" to sell his product lines.

SELF-DESIGNATION

O, he knew what he was

doing—which was filling a need in the life of cat owners and their cats. But what could he call himself? The word "entrepreneur" was still in the dictionary. You'll be surprised to know the designation he used on one of his early business cards. it was: *Edward Lowe, RAMROD.*

If you know that a ramrod is used to ram the explosive charge of a muzzle-loading firearm to prepare it to fire—you will appreciate the title he chose for himself.

Ed was an outdoorsman. He was and remains at home with trees and fields, the growing things and the workings of nature. One of the features to attract his attention was the "tap root" of a tree. Every tree has one. He investigated. He found that in the world of trees the tap root system consists of the main primary roots and the fibrous root system. Its function is to search and find water and dissolve minerals from the surrounding soil in order to feed the tree and guarantee its growth. Kill the tap root and you kill the tree...

This discovery fascinated Ed. Especially the *power* of that tap root! Despite the slenderness and delicate structure of the root tendrils, their myriad number and the spiralling thrust of their energy *is enough to split solid rock!* Here was the organ of growth—the equivalent in human biology of the "growth cell." It was easy for him to make the next logical connection: the tap root and growth cell of the economy is "the entrepreneur." The

entrepreneurial spirit is the spirit of innovation, of enterprise and discovery.

CHOOSES "CELL" UNIT

In 1980, Ed Lowe made this statement, "I conceived the Cell System as the ultimate of fair profit distribution, the base for brain-powered direction, a center for innovative construction of progress melted together with a strong financial base."

He chose "the cell" because *"it is the smallest structural unit of an organism that is capable of independent functioning."* It has initiative. It has energy. It has the inbuilt motivation to grow and do things. It can make decisions. And he saw the human prototype of that basic cell as our fancy-titled friend—*the entrepreneur.*

At last, Ed knew what he was. He knew how he was fitted within the complicated mechanism of the economic pattern. How others like him were also so fitted. He began to conceptualize the structure of a business organization that was a *living body,* not a lawyer's blueprint.

NEED FOR SUPPORT

He studied his own history—what he had done, where he had failed, what his strengths and weaknesses were. He knew that every cell had a *nucleus.* That nucleus was its heart and brain. And it was surrounded by the shield of a *cytoplasm.* The nucleus control center had that cytoplasm as its *support system,* its source for nourishment.

Ed knew that he had been an entrepreneur and that his point of vulnerability had always been the lacking of a cytoplasm. With this realization, he began to design a "cell system" which would reinforce the growth dynamics of the entrepreneurial spirit.

This is like nothing you have ever read or heard before. It is an approach to business organizational systems as *natural, living, healthy organisms.* Most of you have known why the free enterprise economy is the best and most productive system (which is what the ex-Soviet countries are now finding out) but very few have taken the trouble to understand *why.* What is the *vital heart* of the free enterprise system? And how can we nurture and protect that heart?

That's what Ed Lowe was concerned with. He is and always has been a creative thinker, an inventor, innovator and entrepreneur. Out of his own experiences he has evolved this original concept of what makes our economy tick. He calls it *"The Cell System",* and that's what this series of columns in all about. Fasten your seat belt...

Let's start with things you are familiar with. Take "the chip"—the microchip which runs your watch or your P.C. and lots of good things.

A chip is a tiny slice of thin semiconducting material (such as silicon) on which are implanted (or "printed") electric circuits with thousands of tiny components interconnected to perform certain given functions. That chip, you will agree, is a miracle of high technology. It is quite an achievement. *But it is nothing at all when compared to the living cell in biology.*

You've heard of DNA, haven't you? Although I doubt you can spell its full name, which is *Deoxyribonucleic Acid.*

DNA is the genetic code deal, and it has a terrific job to do. It has to define *you,* before your birth, including all your physical characteristics. But consider this: *the microchip is 500,000 times bigger than the living cell!*

The smallest unit in our biology is the cell. It is the basic building block. Some are bigger than others. The smallest cell in human biology is the male sperm-cell. The largest is the female ovum. But there is a common structure for all cells— each has a *nucleus* and a *cytoplast.* The nucleus is the energy source or motor of the cell and directs its activity. The cytoplast protects, nourishes and supports the nucleus, which seems fair enough, doesn't it?

There are approximately a quadrillion cells in the human body. That's 1,000,000,000,000,000. That's what the books say; I haven't had time to count them myself. Which makes the human body a giant apparatus in its own right, to be composed of all these billions of miniaturized units—*cells all tuned in harmony with the total organism.*

Some folks may argue with me, and not give much credit to those tiny little things. "After all," they may tell me, "those cells are all directed by one dominant centralized control—*the brain.*"

C'mon! Where did the brain come from? Those cells had to build all the organs of the body, including the brain. You might say they started from scratch, with the DNA or the genetic "chip" as their blueprint.

To understand this novel notion of Ed Lowe's "cell system" of business organization, you have to discard your ideas of "bigness". We have become overloaded with the appetite to become the biggest; duped into believing that *"the biggest is the best"*. No way. "Miniaturization" is what led us to the microchip, which produced "The Silicon Age" of high-tech electronics. If you are ready to think of a company or corporation as a living, *organic* body, then you'll come along with us as we try to identify *its* basic building block. What is the "cell" of a business?

Get ready for this! A man or woman, or a group of them, starts a company and they decide to "incorporate". You've probably done that yourself. *You formed a corporation.* What is that? A corporation is created under law as an ARTIFICIAL PERSON. That makes it a legal entity separate from the individuals who compose it. It exercises, *like a*

"natural person", the powers that are conferred on it by law.

So, as you knew, that is a corporate body. But, hold on! What happened to the *"natural body"*—the living entity made up of real-life people? Has it been obliterated by the artificial entity fabricated by the lawyers?

It's still there, and you'd better believe it! That's where Ed Lowe discovered the "cell".

The first obligation is to recognize the difference between a living company and an artificial company. When this is understood you are ready to grasp "organic economics" as opposed to "inorganic". You will be able to distinguish *cellular business structures* from the dead weight corporate structures which kill individuality, suppress innovation and disenfranchise the entrepreneur.

Remember this: Ed Lowe's "Cell System" is not aimed at reforming or disturbing the corporate structure of major companies. Its objective is pure and simple: to protect, preserve and help prosper the entrepreneurial spirit, its mission is expressed in three words: *Hail the entrepreneur!*®

HISTORICAL REVIEWS

Let's look at the history of corporations as such. During the 16th and 17th centuries, business corporations took the form of great trading companies. They were vital instruments for entrepreneurial pursuits.

They made possible voyages of discovery, commerce and colonization. (The Christopher Columbus story is a brilliant illustration.) The first English settlements in Virginia and New England came from such trading companies. They were brave, adventurous and creative enterprises.

After the American Revolution of 1776, a quarter million immigrants went Westward over the mountains and in 25 years the original states had chartered more than 300 business organizations in order to facilitate this expansion. The "corporation" now began to settle down and take on a new nature...

It wasn't long before the company's entrepreneurial spirit was being buried by lawyers, accountants and government clerks. The business enterprise was soon established as *"a fictitious legal person."* By 1875, the corporation was looked upon more as a right than as a privilege.

RIGHTS OF CITIZENS

It was the 14th Amendment to the U.S. Constitution which was broadened in interpretation to do the job. This is the amendment which covers *"The Rights of Citizens."* Now, *all* citizens are persons. Remember that the Corporation, while not a citizen as such, is in fact *"an artificial person."*

The Supreme Court then decided that the Corporation is entitled to the protection of the 14th Amendment as a person! Although a corporation is the creation of government, the court ruled, the government may not take the life of a corporate property without the due process of law which is the right of all citizens.

This was good, in that it somewhat restrained the government from interfering too badly in private property. It was bad, in the sense that it rendered corporations even farther removed from the living tissue and heart of the people involved.

After this, it was no surprise that the Corporation developed a "personality". The great companies of America came to be personified as a kind of folk hero. This continues to this day, even though we are in the era of the "shell" or "hollow" corporation, and many a bankrupted shareholder has wallpapered his shack with worthless stock certificates.

How to revive that valiant instrument for free enterprise which started America going? Ed Lowe reckoned that you build a building from the ground up. In his eyes, the foundation, the growth nucleus, was the entrepreneur. If he looked at the needs of that living person and wanted to provide an organic structure to serve those needs—how could it be done?

It needed a cell system—and that's why he designed one.

A business is getting started. It has a new and useful reason to come into being. The market responds to it and it grows in size and profitability. Is that all there is to it? *Ed Lowe thinks not.*

Life is a matter of *ongoing* growth. When growth stops, the life process (even in a business organization) also withers away. True, most companies may be so imbedded in the marketplace that sheer inertia keeps them going long past their prime. It's that way with certain old executives who stay in office because they own stock. It's that way with stars, where we see the light long after the star is burned-out.

Dead or dying companies sooner or later clog up the economy. Like a cancerous growth they tend to enlarge themselves in order to make up for their lack of vitality. They resort to mergers and takeovers, piracy and cutthroat competition, diluting their products and unfair practices. Worst of all, their employees become antagonistic to the owners because they have lost all the loyal enthusiasm that the company generated at the beginning.

You cannot start a business with a genuinely creative idea and then put that idea in cold storage, expecting to retain its energy or its vital spark.

"Every step along the way," Ed says, "is going to demand more new ideas and imaginative applications of the old idea. If the growth cell is locked up in a typical company structure, that company is going to run out of ideas. It's going to wither away. The *yahbutts* will have taken over. The bottomliners and the assets managers will all be looking out of the rearview mirror. They will be studying where they used to be and nobody will be looking for the road ahead."

NOTE: In Ed's parlance, the idea-makers in the business world are the innovators. They are forever proposing a new solution to a problem by suggesting, "What if" (Meaning "What if we did such-and-such"). The Nay-Sayers invariably shoot it down with their immediate reaction, "Yeah, but—" (Meaning "There is no way it will work") So they are the "Yahbutts."

In order to keep the "growth cell" alive and kicking in the design of a business organization, Ed Lowe developed "The Cell System" that will deal with the following problems:

1. The creative force of the entrepreneurial spirit comes from its individuality. Its uniqueness. Its free-wheeling spontaneity. It is unhampered by the lockstep mentality where Ike-and-Mike, they-think-alike. This must be protected.

2. The most vulnerable weakness of the individual entrepreneur comes from *isolation*. Loneliness and lack of support. Being cut off from friendly advisors and the available wisdom of experience. This must be corrected.

3. The first thing "The Cell System" does is to establish a work-

ing environment which affords the entrepreneur free rein for individual creativeness, but offers sponsors, mentors and friendly alliances. This is the first requirement.

UNDERSTAND YOUR HORSE!

That is only the foundation. "One thing the entrepreneur cannot afford," Ed warns "is to be a 'Johnny-One-Note'. If his business, for example, is a horse, he must know how to breed it, feed it, groom it, harness it, ride it, work it and when the time comes to trade it. If he knows only a part of the deal, the horse is going to die or somebody is going to steal it."

The cellular structure knows that a thriving business is operated on an all-out basis—the owner-manager knows its workings from top to bottom.

The apprentice entrepreneur is cushioned or reinforced in the Cell System by a formation of like-minded mentors—composed of successful entrepreneurs. *"It takes one to know one!"*—according to Ed. The owner-manager is encouraged to express his individuality but he is not abandoned to a maverick isolation. He has the reservoir of the "Cell Service Center." This is his arsenal or library from which he can draw the knowledge and techniques to meet his utility needs.

These are: bookkeeping, accounting, taxes, insurance, real estate acquisition, personnel administration, sources of supply, *including the fun-makers and the common-sensers.*

Sooner or later every young growing company runs out of gas and needs a financial transfusion. *This is a historical inevitability.* The living business needs money to keep up with its own growth. Perhaps 8 out of 10 fall on their face because they don't have a banker to turn to when they need it. And they don't know how to talk to that banker if they did have one on hand. The Lowe System provides what is called *"The Central Bank Of Progress."*

Little minds worship bigness. So does cancer. The giant conglomerates (where one bankrupt-prone company is piled on top of another) form great mega-structures, proud of being "the biggest". When mergers, acquisitions and take-overs dominate the scene, you can be sure there's trouble in the counting-house. Misery loves company.

When entrepreneurs dare to start up their independent firms, and family-owned businesses are prospering, you can be certain the economy is growing.

The Age of the Dinosaurs is over! The theme of the day is: *miniaturization. Decentralize—* don't jam it all together. Release creative *initiative*—don't bury it in a crowd of junior clerks. This is the philosophy behind Ed Lowe's "Cell System," which recently won international recognition with a Rolex award.

When the Indians were attacking and the settlers were in grave danger, John Wayne had to call out, *"Pull all the wagons into a circle!"* *(Never circle the wagons into a dollar ($) sign.)* But when the coast was clear and homesteaders were roaring out to stake their claims, it was *"Westward Ho!"* and each wagon was hellbent for breakfast.

There are various ways to illustrate the basic principle of the Cell System. One way is complicated but very dramatic. In electronics and microphysics, the successful trend has been toward miniaturization. Getting inside the atom has been the challenge of the last half-century. Nuclear physics has moved into the interior of the atom to become "particle physics." Among other discoveries, once this was achieved, we had "The Big Bomb" on our hands, because the energy inside the atom had been triggered to explode.

In every field of science and scientific management, attention has gone toward *de-centralizing,* locating the most efficient, elementary unit of operation.

—Except in the world of business! In business affairs the trend has been toward **giantism**, hoping the immensity of the coalition can hide the inherent bankruptcy of the separate entities.

As the corporate structures went up, productivity went down.

In physics the exciting new developments are coming from work with the *leptons and the quarks*—the particles inside the world of the atom. In business, the growth perspective will come from nurturing the *cell,* the energy source for business dynamics.

Ed Lowe searched through the years of his own entrepreneurial experience trying to find the ways and means for improving his own operations. Where was his strength? Where was his weakness? What he found was the *vital core* of any enterprise—the creative motor force, as it was personified in the entrepreneur. Its problem was that it needed to be nourished and allowed to function freely and fully. So around that core he drew an organizational format—the matrix, and thus was born *the cell system.*

This is the heart of *organic economics*—the living substance of a business organization.

(RE-PRINTED FROM EDWARD LOWE'S MAIN STREET JOURNAL - 1989)

DISCUSSING THE ENTREPRENEUR AS A "TAP ROOT"

Every self-styled "expert" on the subject talks about "the economic system" as if it were a cut-and-dried abstraction (something out of a text book.) They make it sound as if the "economy" was a set of tracks that the train of production and commerce runs on—as if the whole business is a *mechanical* rig of some sort.

The Edward Lowe "Cell System" (which won an international award from Rolex in 1989) is based on a very fundamental assumption, easy enough to understand:

THE ECONOMY IS ALIVE

"Economics" is the way living people live, work and prosper with-each other. It is a natural process and the laws of nature affect it as they do all living things, including mankind.

Some economic systems are better than others. Some live and some die. All systems are subject to disease, to old age and to malnutrition. There's really nothing mysterious about economics except the mystery the professional economists conjure up. They talk about economic "laws and trends" as if they came out of the blue, ordained by the heavens, when in fact they all are developed in a natural way by the human beings who practice such tendencies.

"Capitalism" is not a dirty word. But it has been made to sound cold and dehumanized. It happens to be a title conceived of by theoreticians. All it means is that the funds (forms of wealth) which are useful for activating new ventures are called "capital". There's nothing ugly about that.

But then it turns everybody who operates with such investment funds into "capitalists". The Marxists, the cartoonists and assorted radicals have turned that image into a bloated plutocrat wearing a tall silk hat. This all feeds the *"Soak the Rich"* compaigns.

They hate to use the real term for a market economy. That term is "free enterprise" and the problem there is that the words "free" and "enterprise" are *beautiful* words. If you will notice the changes going on in the broken-up Soviet Union and in China, the official description of what's happening in those countries, getting free of totalitarian chains, is called "a return to the market system". For obvious reasons they hate to call it a "free enterprise operation", or going back to capitalism—although that's what it is, or what it is trying to be.

Repeat: an economic system is a living organism. To keep alive it has to *grow*. When growth stops, life stops. That is the natural law. *Freedom to grow is the basic freedom of all freedoms*. It is the freedom that built America's greatness.

When a living body is constrained in a strait jacket which prevents movement and growth, that body suffers pain and cramping and eventually wastes away.

In the same way, when the growth cells, the dynamic units of the living body, are starved, or suffocated or amputated, *the whole organism suffers,* and sooner or later must expire.

Edward Lowe's discovery that the entreprenur is the growth cell (or tap root) of the living economy was a *major* revelation.

In the first place, it *personifies* the nuclear dynamics of the economic system. For the first time we can identify the germinating forces for growth in our economy. We know it isn't some financial manipulator such as a J.P. Morgan. We can spot the actual people (such as Ed Lowe) who are the core of our economic growth. We can begin identifying the living growth cell of the free enterprise environment.

With the "funnel vision" afforded by this concept, Edward Lowe raised the warning cry, *"The entrepreneur is an endangered species.* HAIL ENTREPRENEUR!®

"Hail" means "good health"—it signifies encouragement and reinforcement to the entrepreneur who is in danger of being terminated in today's unhealthy situation.

"Hail Entrepreneur" is more than a cheer-leading exercise. *The Lowe theory of a living economy is a full-bodied philosophy dedicated to the preservation of the growth cells.*

The theory is practiced in a practical program of therapy and revival. A warning is not enough. A *plan* needs to be brought into action to ward off the danger, strengthen the entrepreneurial spirit and restore the health of the entire economy. Edward Lowe and his Foundation are chartered for exactly this crusade.

If the free enterprise system is to remain free it must re-establish its freedom to grow. The power to grow depends on the ongoing health and stamina of the growth cells—those individual entrepreneurs who act as the tap roots and pathfinders for the economy.

The Edward Lowe "Cell System" in practice is a mutual insurance system which can serve to reinforce the weak or vulnerable aspects of the entrepreneur's growing power. It begins with a diagnosis of these unprotected areas:

1. Isolation: The "loner" syndrome which customarily cuts off the entrepreneur from sympathetic counseling.

2. Ignorance: the lack of information and access to necessary data which keeps the entrepreneur in the dark.

3. Indebtedness: The usual danger of under-capitalization and difficulty obtaining loans and lines of credit.

All of these remedies are provided in the Cell System—ranging from Mentors to the Bank of Progress.

It must be remembered that the *heart* of the system is the growth cell which justifies the protective shell. That is the *creative, active, well-applied energy of the entrepreneur,* the owner-operator of the enterprise. Based on that cell, the system is designed to ensure its growth and save it from oppressive forces.

Where does such a System come from? How is it organized? Who are the Mentors? Who are the Co-

Investors? How are potential Entrepreneurs attracted to this System?

The Edward Lowe credo contends that *all successful entrepreneurs* have a stake in the survival of the free enterprise system, and the nurturing of the coming generation of entrepreneurs. In effect, his Foundation is asking his peers, as a WagonMaster might call out when an Indian attack is on the way!

"Pull all your wagons in a circle! Prepare to defend your family and your lives!" He didn't say pull into a dollar sign.

It's no joke. Today's situation is as life-threatening as an Indian attack on a wagon train. The peril is frightening. It happens that so much of the bounty of American enterprise is on hand, and so many successful enterprisers are extant, that their collaboration in the "Cell System" can be worthy and rewarding.

This is not a charity benefit. All participants in a Cell System endeavor will profit from interactions. On the other hand if the Cell System principle doesn't become operational, the American Dream may turn into a nightmare of despair.

Post Script:

The entrepreneur is the key item in this plan. How will he or she be chosen? Edward Lowe has the answer to that...

"They will choose themselves!" he tells us. "You don't have to teach a beagle to chase rabbits. He has a built-in desire to do it. And so do the entrepreneurial types who aspire to succeed in their own businesses."

The System doesn't want any candidates who think they may some day want to be an entrepreneur, or who vaguely believe they have such a potential.

The bonafide entrepreneur will have already proven his or her credentials by having launched some enterprise with some success. That doesn't mean that such an enterprise is fully established or not in trouble. It means that a start-up has been made, and that Cell System Mentors will be able to recognize an entrepreneur who is worthy of the reinforcement the Cell System can offer.

As this book goes to press the Edward Lowe Foundation is testing an unusual facility called *"The Entrepreneur's Development Track"*. Its purpose is to provide a screening-advisory system for individual entrepreneurs to be interrogated, encouraged to express their growth-problems and to receive counsel and direction from experienced mentors.

The "Track" is an "assembly line" process where the candidate moves from room to room where he or she has quality-time with specialists, in everything from accounting to advertising, operations to personnel, etc. As pioneer efforts have demonstrated, this "track" shows signs of offering a concentrated accelerated awareness-enhancing course to prospective entrepreneurs, novice entrepreneurs and entrepreneurs in need of specialized counsel.

The "Track", as it is refined in successive rehearsals may be able to "turn out" as many as six candidates in a two-day cycle—serviced by six mentors.

Edward Lowe, the founder of the system, gave it high marks.

"We've got some bugs to work out," he said, "but we're coming up with something brand new and with high efficiency for the welfare of the entrepreneur."

NOTE: At the end of this book you'll find the Edward Lowe "Self Evaluation Profile Interrogator" which will help you answer the question "Am I an Entrepreneur?"

SECTION THREE

WHAT HISTORY MEANS TO US

Introduction,

In the olde nursery story, Hansel and Gretel kept track of their trail in the Black Forest by dropping cookie crumbs.

In the same way, our forefathers have dropped scraps of paper so that we don't lose **our** way. There they are—The Magna Carta, the Mayflower Compact, the Declaration of Independence, the Emancipation Proclamation. They were all brilliant, God-inspired, memorialized documents. They led us this far...

Now it is time for **us** to drop a new piece of paper of our own...

A LONG LOOK AT HISTORY

For centuries past
the thing that lasts
is the cause of liberty

Now to find what is true
it is time to review
the history that set us free

From barons of old
in England bold
to Mayflower's sworn decree

Don't forget the page
from that valiant age
when America set itself free

Or when thousands fell
to the tolling bell
over Gettysburg's fallen dead

Our History's book
takes more than a look
it is lived much more than read

Heed the lasting laws
the gees and haws
of teams that had to clash

Remember that our dead
bravely died and bled
for love and not for cash

—*Edward Lowe*

LESSONS OF HISTORY

Man can make his own history, but he must do it with the tools provided by history.

My confrontation with Don Quixote and his book opened my eyes to many things. I have seen how our history has been celebrated by *pieces of paper* from the Magna Carta to the Emancipation Proclamation, as we progressed from peonage to liberation.

It looks to me that most of man's achievements have taken place and left their mark on "The Paper Trail". The "Brick Wall" obstacles which have popped up to block Progress along the way have all in their time been overcome by historic documents recording *"the demolition of the walls."*

Of course there were flesh-and-blood heroes (men and women) behind each monumental scroll of those historical documents.

Now it is up to us and the coming generations to carry on with the fight for progress.

America needs us. History is waiting for us.

Writing a great document is quite a thing to do, of course. But all those historic pieces of paper would have been trash if they hadn't been signed! Words are necessary, but it takes human courage to give them voice.

History can't do a thing without us!

SING ALONG PROUDLY

PRIDE JACK PRIDE
We got to get
Our country back
We got to get our
Country back, Jack.

We got to get
Our wheels a turnin'
Got to get our
Guts to churnin'.

Got to get our
Country back, Jack.
We got to get our
Urge to *win* back.

Got to get the urge
To win back, Jack.

To win at knowing
The land is ours,
The roots grow deep
In all the flowers.

We got to win
The land back, Jack.
Got to get
Our pride back
Got to get our
Pride back, Jack.

We got to light
Our sense of pride
Got to get
That "feel" inside.

GOT TO GET THE PRIDE BACK, JACK!

ED LOWE
LOOKS AT HISTORY

> 1. **The Great Paper Trail**
> 2. **The Mountain Man**
> 3. **The Dragon-Killer**

As a boy, I didn't have the slightest notion of what was meant by "History". For all I knew, it was just something that happened a long time ago. Or maybe it was a museum where old things were stored.

Later on I began thinking of "History" as sort of a circus parade. It was exciting and I kept my eye on it looking for things and people I might recognize.

Then one day I got the surprise of my life when I suddenly spotted somebody I knew!

It was me!

That's how I found out that "History" is a parade, sure enough. And everyone of us is in it. Which is why we should pay close attention to it. Take a look at these bits of History as I see them. They all tell a story which could be important to your life and to your good fortune.

Is the parade going our way?

"Civilized man has left a paper trail throughout his history marking his greatest efforts in the ongoing struggle for liberation"

The Documentation of Civilized Man's *Candidacy For Greatness*

1225
MAGNA CARTA
"Liberation from Autocracy"

1620
MAYFLOWER COMPACT
"Liberation from Tyranny"

1776
DECLARATION OF INDEPENDENCE
"Liberation from Colonialism"

1876
EMANCIPATION PROCLAMATION
"Liberation from Human Slavery"

NOW! it is time for a New Charter of Liberty for Free Enterprise!

THE BRICK WALL THEORY OF HISTORY

The history of mankind, as we read it, is a story of trying to make life better. That's part of it. The other part is the appearance of "brick walls" to block that progress. Then there is a third part—that's the spurt of energy that enables the forward movement of mankind to get through that brick wall which is blocking his way.

This is a theory of history that's pretty hard to argue with. We can trace it in our own lives, in the lives of our parents, grandparents and others in the family tree, as far back as we can count it. Everybody was trying to *get ahead*. That's what we called "progress"—*making life better.*

Once you get down to brass tacks, that's what our history is all about, the effort from generation to generation to lift ourselves a wee bit more above the *teeth of the tiger.* (The "tiger" is scarcity, hunger, and deprivation. You know the scare that can give us.)

But "History" like any great effort runs into trouble. There is always some rain on the parade. You solve this problem or that problem and Wham—you run into a *brick wall.* Forward movement gets baffled. It looks like the game is over. Instead of going ahead, getting better and all that, your home and family, your town and nation—everything starts to slide backward. The brick wall is

doing you in.

It takes time. You suffer a lot of trouble and confusion. There's a lot of milling around. And then the parade starts to re-group itself. New leaders stand up. Somebody says: *"What is this brick wall made of?"*

Everybody looks at it, brick after brick. Somebody says, "Hey! This wall is made up out of greed. Just doggonned *greed!"* Then a champion comes along and says, *"I think if we stick together we can get over that brick wall."*

The Documentation of Civilized Man's Candidacy for Greatness has left a Paper Trail.

Mankind trudges along in the mud of everyday toil, but in rare moments of greatness his flight to posterity is memorialized...*in a piece of paper!*

What was the great Charter of Engish Liberty?

It was *The Magna Carta, 1225.*

Granted by Henry III in 1225 under threat of civil war by 25 Barons.

☆Demanding a free church, free elections, reform of inheritance taxes, easing of taxation, outlawing the arrest of free men.

☆A battlecry against royal oppression, weakening the "divine right of kings" opening the door to the Modern Age.

HISTORIC "FIRSTS"

The first voluntary allegiance to a Government for "The General Good"!

The first permanent colony in America, setting the stage for democracy-to-come.

What was the *Declaration of Independence*?

The unanimous declaration of the original 13 United States of America, July 4, 1776.

Declaring that they were *"free and of a right ought to be free and independent states..."*

To this piece of paper, the signers did *"Pledge our lives, our fortunes and our sacred honor."* and in so doing they pledged the lives, fortunes and honor of future citizens. **(It becomes our pledge, too.)**

What was the *Mayflower Compact*?

It was a covenant or contract signed by 41 pilgrims after a 66-day voyage in a little 90-foot sailing vessel over stormy seas, pledging...

"to combine ourselves together in a civil body politic to enact just and equal laws for the general good of the colony..."

What was the *Emancipation Proclamation*?

In the midst of a very bloody civil war on January 1, 1863, President Lincoln issued an executive order ordering to all states...

"All persons held as slaves... shall be free then, thenceforward and forever free."

Considered to be a crucial factor in the Union victory, and called by Lincoln (in his own words) *"The greatest event in the 19th Century."*

And so the U.S.A. came to universal suffrage, popular democracy and the industrial age. Where do we go from here?

THIS IS THE FELLOW WHO OPENED THE DOOR

...When I disovered "The Mountain Men" it opened the door to my understanding of American History...

They were the intrepid hunters and fur trappers who explored the entire West in the generation after the Revolution of 1776—from 1790 to 1830.

When I read their history I was ready to dispense with the old mythical "heroes" like Buffalo Bill and Kit Carson. These Mountain Men were the real giants who developed the plains and mountain survival crafts that settlers, gold miners and cowboys would need later on.

They were the frontrunners, moving into the wilderness as self-reliant individuals, living off the land, earning their own keep, meeting the Indian tribes and learning their languages and habits.

They had to know the laws of Nature, battle the elements and track the game they were after.

When I discovered these Mountain Men I knew I was meeting blood brothers. I recognized that they were the bonafide entrepreneurs who blazed the trail for the opening of the continent. They did so not with guns and armies, but with their own courage, their own wits and their remarkable individualism.

SALUTE TO THE MOUNTAIN MAN
By Edward Lowe

*His appearance was one of
  indescribable view.
His knowledge of Nature was
  extended to two.
Who was this rarity who
  solved the Savage's gap?
A fellow whose learning was
  from the snap of a trap.
He was rugged, resourceful,
  undeniably bold.
Grass roots to much deeper
  when reaching for gold.
In cold streams where fate
  could be found in a pan
Hail Entrepreneur to the
  brave Mountain Man!*

Facing small business

Published by the Edward Lowe Foundation

TAXES

(1) It is the complexity of taxation, as much as the volume, which burdens small business excessively.

(2) The proliferation of taxation entities at state as well as federal levels, creates an untenable demand on small businesses for management's time as well as money.

(3) Increasing taxes directly undermine a small business' ability to expand and create new jobs, and thereby stifles growth in the economy.

REGULATIONS

(1) The inconsistent and inflexible interpretation of constantly changing regulations, by regulations themselves, overwhelms small businesses with extraordinary, unproductive and expensive work to achieve compliance.

(2) The fear of new, even more onerous regulations often deters owners and managers of small business from expanding their businesses.

(3) Small businesses believe they are encumbered disproportionately by regulations which do not distinguish between large and small businesses.

CREDIT AND CAPITAL

(1) Small businesses often find financial institutions willing but unable to provide financing for fear of violating regulations. They are confused by the variety of government loan guarantee programs and the complexity of qualifying for a loan.

(2) There may be a need for a central "clearinghouse," advising and guiding small businesses to the sources of financing (one stop shopping) which would match specific needs with the optimum source for financial service from among the numerous alternatives that exist.

(3) Bankers who would otherwise lend to small business often will not because environmental regulations require them to pay for cleaning contaminated property used as collateral in the event of foreclosure.

HEALTH CARE COSTS

(1) A broader, but affordable health care system is needed, but government's ability to manage and control one is often questioned.

(2) There is a concern that a new health care program may fail to recognize the disparate capacities and needs among small businesses of different types and sizes.

(3) Small businesses often express preference for private sector solutions to the health care problem, and a belief that consumer choice and individual responsibility must be part of any government mandated health care system.

INFORMATION COMMUNICATION TECHNOLOGY

(1) Information and communication technology is an important resource which is still beyond the grasp of small business entrepreneurs who are the most needy.

(2) The need for information could be better met if small businesses could access available information locally.

(3) Small businesses are often unable to access more specialized information because the sources are unknown in public channels.

Hey! Who opened the door?

MAP OF THE
MOUNTAIN MAN'S COUNTRY
THE MODEL TERRAIN
FOR TODAY'S ENTREPRENEURS

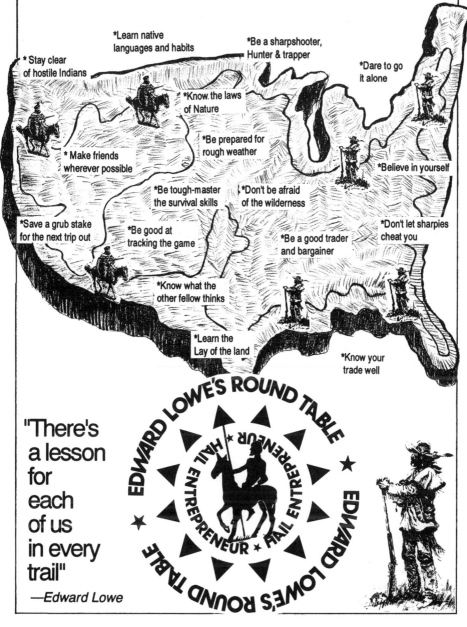

*Learn native languages and habits

*Be a sharpshooter, Hunter & trapper

* Stay clear of hostile Indians

*Dare to go it alone

*Know the laws of Nature

*Be prepared for rough weather

* Make friends wherever possible

*Believe in yourself

*Be tough-master the survival skills

*Don't be afraid of the wilderness

*Save a grub stake for the next trip out

*Be good at tracking the game

*Be a good trader and bargainer

*Don't let sharpies cheat you

*Know what the other fellow thinks

*Learn the Lay of the land

*Know your trade well

EDWARD LOWE'S ROUND TABLE

HAIL ENTREPRENEUR

HAIL ENTREPRENEUR

EDWARD LOWE'S ROUND TABLE

"There's a lesson for each of us in every trail"
—*Edward Lowe*

The Edward Lowe Free Enterprise Theatre Presents:

"Conversation with a Legend"

(Ed Lowe is seated on a bench on the Sunset Walk at Azalea Gardens. He is all by himself, in a quiet, studious mood, watching the sun go down. He is pondering...)

EL: Boy, that theory of history has got me stumped. I know it's right in theory, but where do we go from here? It sure is something to ponder about.

(He looks around)

My problem is this: we're up against some of the biggest brick walls of all time. How do we get over them?

(Looks out at setting sun)

What we need is a champion. You know, a symbolic leader—one we can all feel good about because he stands for *us*. I don't mean a Superman who does things we should be doing for ourselves. I mean an *"Uncommon Man"* He has no extraordinary powers except the spirit and the will to go after all the brick walls that block his way.

(Shakes his head)

Nope. He's not a gigantic figure. He's somewhat on the lean and hungry scale. He might even appear a little silly to some folks...

(In the Western sky he sees a book appear. The title is large and clear: DON QUIXOTE BY CERVANTES, 1605)

EL: It must be a mirage. An optical illusion. I swear I can see a book cover up there!

VOICE: You swear right. The message is coming through.

EL: You mean? You're not—?

VOICE: Yes I am. I am Don Quixote

EL: But you're a *legend!*

VOICE: What's so terrible about legends? Anyone who can see brick walls that aren't really there should be able to do business with a legend.

EL: I'm not knocking legends. As a boy I had King Arthur for one of my heroes. I learned a lot from the legend of his Round Table.

VOICE: Join the club! I, Don Quixote, I dreamed of King Arthur's Round

Table, too. That fired me up to do battle with the dragons. That was my way of being true to a legend.

EL: And what happened to you?

VOICE: I had a thousand glorious adventures. I became famous in every land around the world—to generation after generation for the last 400 years.

EL: It's strange that I imagined I could see your book in the sky. I've been thinking of books. The Bible, of course—the greatest book. And then I thought of King Arthur and how I always wanted to grow up and be a knight.

VOICE: So did I! So did I!

EL: But King Arthur is only a legend! Legends exist only in your mind!

VOICE: Which is why they are so powerful Your mind is the most powerful resource you have. Don't put down the power of your mind and the power of legends. They can handle real-life things like brick walls...

EL: *(Looking at camera)*

I've been sitting here pondering trying to conjure up a champion for our cause. We needed a champion who was as bewildered as us, but his example can show us that we can stand up and tell the forces that built all these brick walls— *"That's enough!"*

VOICE: You have got it straight! Those brick walls are no tougher than my dragons. We can break'em down!

EL: Would you...? I mean are you willing to be our wall-banger?

(He looks down toward the bench where he sees the figure of a knight on horseback.)

VOICE: Hail entrepreneur! Let's put this show on the road!

(The figure of Don Quixote slowly fades from the sky. Ed sits there pondering.)

EL: I guess I dreamed that one up, didn't I? Don Quixote's been out of date for almost 400 years. What makes me think my imagination can revive him now, just because we need a champion to be a symbol for us now?

VOICE: (from distance) Hail-l-l-l-l Entre-pre-neurrrrr!

EL: Well, I dreamed up Kitty Litter so it become a standard part of the language. If we're going to revive the entrepreneur, it shouldn't be too much trouble to revive Don Quixote.

(He stands and waves to sky)

OK, DQ! we're putting this show in the road!

(We hear rapid hoof beats of a galluping horse and then the crashing sound of a brick wall collapsing.)

EL: Call it fantasy if you want to, but there was a brick wall that took old Don Quixote seriously and that brick wall came tumbling down.

FADE OUT

HERE HE COMES!!!

Defender of Small Businesses, Champion of Free Enterprise, Cradle of the Entrepreneur, Cornerstone of American Prosperity.

400 years ago the great Spanish writer Cervantes created a heroic character—***Don Quixote*** who dared to attack any dragon he could see. *Where is our Don Quixote today?*

own "Magna Carta"

Because. Wonderful document that it is, in its time and place, *The U.S. Constitution* protects *individual persons* but its provisions do not cover the welfare of Small Business, in this era of giant corporatism.

Our Constitution, however, does indeed grant citizens (such as ourselves) the right to arm our modern day Don Quixote with a current "Bill

Who will break down that Brick Wall Maze?

Why does "The Little Guy" of today's business world need his

of Rights" in the form of this Charter which itemizes our grievances and our demand for relief.

HEY THERE-DRAGON-KILLER!

Are you there,
my Don Quixote?
Is your steed
shod and true?

Does Sancho believe
you are the fool
who jousts with mills
with inadequate tool?

Many times dragons
look like mills
to fool our senses
weaken our wills

Quoth the wise ones,
"There's nothing there!
You're probing spears
at empty air!"

But we see clearly
what must fall—
It's not the dragon,
It's that brick wall!

So charge, Don Quixote!
Break down the wall!
We behind you
will heed your call!

—*Edward Lowe*

Does your signature mean anything?

TODAY'S MAGNA CARTA

Charter of Liberty

FOR FREE ENTERPRISE

CARRY ON "THE PAPER TRAIL"!

WILL YOU SIGN THIS CHARTER?

We the free and independent pathfinders of the fertile American economy, being sovereign citizens dedicated to our Nation's growth and progress, loyal to our heritage of hard work, honest dealings and fair rewards for venturesome effort do hereby address and petition our elected representatives in all government offices in the following regards:

•**FOR THE QUICK AND THOROUGH RELEASE** of our cramping entrepreneurial energies so that germinal small, independently-owned enterprises may fruitfully engage in the initiative, innovation and experimentation which have been the hallmark of America's unrivaled development.

• **FOR THE SORELY-NEEDED UNBURDENING** of such small business enterprises from the crippling effects of bureaucratic harassment, counterproductive rules and uncalledfor restrictions and coercive regulations.

• **FOR MERCIFUL RELIEF FROM EXCESSIVE TAXATION** and arbitrary penalties, including relief from the punitive costs of government overhead which has been swollen by extravagance, waste, special privilege and corrupt practices.

• **FURTHERMORE IN SUPPORT OF THESE PROVISIONS**, we ask for an Executive Order to redefine "Small Business" as constructed by public policy and to identify it in all governmental interactions as *any and all firms engaged in profit-seeking commerce, employing fewer than one hundred employees* and generating *less than one million dollars per annum* in after-tax revenues.

• **WE PROPOSE IN THE IMPLEMENTATION OF THIS CHARTER** that a Federal Department of Small Business Free Enterprise be established which shall be staffed to oversee and arbitrate all grievances and complaints in its jurisdiction and which shall be accorded a *Secretary of Small Business,* seated in the Presidential Cabinet.

• **WE STRONGLY PLEAD THAT ALL NEW BUSINESS ENTERPRISES** covered under the redefined Small Business Code shall be granted tax exemption for the critical start-up period of their first twelve months of operation, and that such enterprises independently owned and operated be granted enabling legislation which will provide them low interest loans and lines of credit endorsed by the U.S. Treasury.

In support of these demands and solicitations we hereby set our names and pledge our backing. HAIL ENTREPRENEUR!®

WHY I SHUTTLE BETWEEN BIG ROCK VALLEY

(Cassopolis, Michigan)

AND E & D CATTLE RANCH

(Arcadia, Florida)

History is a growing thing. We are all growing things, being nourished by the land, and helping change the land.

It's not that I'm a land hog. (Somebody once said that I only want the land that's next to mine.) But I confess, *I do very much believe in the land.*

Land is the foundation for our life on earth. If a growing thing loses its roots in the land, it is no longer growing. A tree pulled out of the ground is no longer a tree—it's lumber.

The good fortune that has been mine has all come out of the earth—clay for Kitty Litter and paper for Biodac®. A great deal of that fortune has been used to pull a lot of beautiful land together and improve it for a good purpose. Let me explain what I've been up to...

First of all, I never went after land that somebody wanted to hold onto. Almost entirely, I acquired acreage that was not being used. If and when some land next to mine became available, I'd make a bid for it. I started pulling Big Rock Valley together in 1950, not really knowing what I would do with it. It happened to be the locale of my boyhood as well as the place of origin of my company. I loved it and that was the beginning of what we have now.

Secondly, because I believe in the land, and because I learned a lot about land acquisition in my many years of commercial dealings in more than a few states—I have become a pretty savvy judge of land. I have wanted only beautiful land, land that could be treated better and which I was ready to improve considerably.

Along the way my attention was turned to Florida. The acreage north of Arcadia started with a purchase from a family that disagreed on the future operation of the land.

Darlene and I were in close agreement, although my management team had doubts. We continued to accumulate land around the original purchase, upgrading the cattle, adding orange groves, living quarters and accommodations to our liking.

Our feeling is that the land serves to frame our vision of the future. We believe that land can become immensely important if it is thought of and managed as an *important* asset—not a drudge or a liability.

It isn't a matter of simple geography. America, in terms of its landscape, is grandly beautiful from coast to coast and border to border. I wouldn't argue with anyone who thinks of their homegrounds, wherever they may be, as the most beautiful in the country. Or the world. I have my taste and you have yours.

Michigan and Florida as far as I'm concerned, represent a North Pole and a South Pole of our purely American "world". In every way, color, composition and season, they make a dandy contrast. It's a matter of history, climate and culture. If you wanted a pair of places which ranked as being beauties but were two *different* **worlds** that's what Big Rock Valley and our Cattle Ranch signified to Darlene and me.

Between the two of them, we've got the richness, the grandeur and the bedrock base of America the beautiful. Or so I think.

Another question I run into is: *why so much land?* Why so *many* acres? Almost 6,000 acres all told.

Well, land as God and Nature intended, has sort of a "family" sense to it. There's such a thing as "composition" in the natural configuration of a spread or a terrain. So much "belongs" together. This involved the sweep and the scope of the land, its contiguous neighbors, waterways, rills and rises, the roads of access and numerous other factors.

In Michigan, it has a lot to do

with the history of the place. It is old country with its traditions involving Indians, the Civil War and the Underground Railroad and the Industrial Revolution. We own a baker's dozen of landmark farmhouses there (over 100 years old) which we've restored to mint condition.

What's more, the great glaciers of the Ice Age which carved out the Great Lakes dropped an enormous harvest of rocks there. Michigan farmers did a whale of a job clearing the land for cultivation. (We keep watering our rocks so they'll keep on growing.) We call it "our Rock Garden of the North".

What we've got there now is a parkland of breath-taking beauty with ample accommodations and facilities. If you'd ever see it, you'd recognize that its unlike any other place in the world, and it would help explain our presence there.

Florida now is something else. It is truly "the other side of the coin." When the English set out to colonize this continent they called their colonies "plantations". They were planting seeds in the New World. In that sense, we've set up a plantation in the gorgeous acreage near Arcadia.

We've got semi-tropical seasons here. It's a real change of venue—the kind of transformation that invigorates the creative spirit. Big Rock Valley had our purebred Black Horse Stable, while the Florida Ranch has Texas Long Horn Cattle (we've since moved the horses

South). Big Rock has white-tailed deer, fox, eagles and whooping cranes. The Ranch has wild boar, alligators and peacocks.

Here's a descriptive narration we used in a film of the Florida landscape....

GOD IS CLOSER TO US

Stunning secrets of Nature
in luxurious array
spread their arts before our eyes
in this treasurehouse of
Floridian splendor

Here garlands of greenery
and gems of tropical floral
wreaths
vie with the sparkle
of orange trees in delightful
contrast
offering us a tranquil exercise
sensuously bathed
in the rustic beauty of the scene

Immersing us in its embrace
until we know in our hearts
the mystery, the essential secret
which is the ineffable truth
that Nature is the mother of us all
We grow and we are nourished
by the bounty of the earth
by generous soil, by gracious sky
by the benevolence of sun
all the tones and flavors
of the divine palette
This is Nature's gift
the panoramic scope which feeds
our senses
with the nutriments of wonder
displayed in God's scenario

We are restored by its calmness

this serene self-composure
of wilderness which is not wild
where waters run in rills and
streams
following paths they have chosen
where hills ripple and the
meadows
spread like a verdant table
for the grateful trees

Peace is growing here
midst the concert of the wild grass
the shadowed woods
and the fine lace of growing
things
Peace is nursing here
on Nature's bosom
strengthening goodwill in men
refreshing the city-worn soul
uplifting stressful minds
under the benign surveillance
of radiant sun and cobalt sky

The richness and the lushness
of this privileged land
offers comfort to the crisis-
strained
because within this enclave
buttressed on all sides
by the green armor of the land's
decor
the fragile human psyche
can find fresh pride in its own
being
and God will be closer to us
in this theatre of loveliness
where the blessing of His love
will be more sweetly felt

Why have I invested so heavily in Big Rock Valley and the E&D Cattle Ranch? Because America is a world of unrivaled promise and in these two great properties we have a good foothold in the best of two areas—the North and the South.

To repeat—Darlene and I love the land. Not long ago we all saw the televised report of the Pope's arrival in America. *He knelt down and kissed the soil!* I feel like doing that every day of the year. Even now, when we've come so far, this urge of mine to own undeveloped pristine land is beyond the understanding of many people. This is because they don't share our feeling toward the land. They see land as a burden because it has to be maintained, which, of course it does. I feel that such minds lack vision for the future. They think life starts and is justified with a start-up cash flow. *Cash is king for such mentalities.*

For us, land is the anchor, the seedbed, the foundation for whatever you may have in mind. Let me tell you what I have in mind...

What do you do? You *grow* things on land. That's what land is for. Our continental real estate is a big piece of land. Our America has grown a lot of things on it—cities, farms, highways, families, Disneyland. Some things, of course, are better than others.

Growing things calls for cultivating the land. Cultivation is what produces culture.

My dictionary tells me that cultivation is *"to bestow labor and attention in order to produce or raise a desirable crop."*

It also says that cultivation is "the devoting of attention or study in order to improve or develop by education and training. "

My own particular brand of culture is concerned with the grass roots individual enterpriser in the American economic pattern who has been given the name *"Entrepreneur."*

My interest here is easy enough to understand. The typical "entrepreneur" is a self-starter, stand-alone, go-getter with the stamina to set up a business based on an original idea and make it prosper. *That's what I did.* I'm an entrepreneur and I feel a deep kinship with others of the same cut—past, present and future, too.

The problem is that this type of an economic producer is hardput these days to hold his own, let alone develop in a healthy way. Between the pressure of the giant cartels and the red tape of government bureaucracy, today's entrepreneur is having a very tough time.

Worse than that, the coming generations of young people are being discouraged from following entrepreneurial pursuits.

Independent initiative and the talent for innovation are being smothered by a psychology which is looking for an easy ride with a free lunch and a comfortable pension. The world of Big Business has begun to look like a welfare system.

We've got to do something about this!

This isn't just a sentimental notion of mine. I want to help budding entrepreneurs, but not just for old time's sake. America's free enterprise economy is in trouble—*deep trouble*. The entrepreneurial energy that used to nourish and expand our wealth as a nation is running out.

The ground needs tilling. The economy needs cultivation. And it's to that end that I am dedicating the use of my land.

The land I've developed in Michigan and the ranch in Florida will serve as the North and the South campus for my *American Academy of Entrepreneurs*. Here we are planting all the facilities and accommodations (housing, conference centers, high-tech equipment, etc.) to cultivate the dynamics of the American entrepreneurial spirit.

My Edward Lowe Foundation has a mission, which is available for all to read. This mission is hamstrung due to some brick walls and so the development of the American Academy of Entrepreneurs will be carried on under its own heading.

You don't need to teach a beagle how to chase rabbits. But you can show him where the rabbits can be found. The creative spirit of the wouldbe entrepreneur can be nurtured and expanded in an environment which is conducive to it.

Big Rock Valley and the Cattle Ranch are quite inspiring landsites for our adventure to flower in. It takes a big plot of ground to house a program as big as the one we're working on.

The 21st Century is roaring in on us faster than a freight train, carrying promises, challenges, threats and opportunities by the carload. The U.S.A. and the world are on the threhold of greater adventures.

Do we want to be an innovative, creative, functional part of the excitement? Or do we prefer to lollygog in the security of long term, low-interest bonds of security?

Name your position. We have ours.

TOMORROW IS PLANTED HERE

*My heart is buried in the rooks
  and rills
the billowing hills and secret trails
of Big Rock Valley*

*The bare feet of my boyhood
have bathed in the tall grass here
and I have tracked deer, wild hare
and the wily raccon
I have breathed the sweet air
  of Spring
and the keen whistling snow-
  sprinkled air
of white winter come to Big
  Rock Valley
I came to manhood among
  these trees
and I have planted futures
in the landmark farmhouses,
  one-room schools
and a century-old Quaker church
great old weathered barns
that we've turned into offices,*

research centers
that fine gracious domicile
    "the barnhouse"
and, of course, of course,
the cabin on the brow of the hill

I close my eyes and hear my heart
    remember
the crazy creek, the sugar shack,
the A-Frame and the astonishing
    caboose
all the delights of the woodland, the
    meadows
and the footprints we have
    impressed
midst all this beauty and
    peacefulness

Come again to Billyville
with its frontier look for familiarity
and the amenities of a modern
    retreat
welcoming study, inviting conferees

At rustic Billyville you can sit at
    the bar
and feel very much at home
or use the milti-media facility
to see, hear and think through
    the problems
of today's entrepreneurial
    generation
All around are the landmarks
of our life and our mission planted
    here
in the Casey Jones memorial twenty
    foot high
the dormitories in old boxcars
the Picklebarrel golf course,
the jury room, and a dozen
    Centennial houses

serving as inns and lodging
There it is encamped in tribute
to the pioneer farmers who cleared
    the land

These great rocks are older than the
    hills
and still they breathe
they hunker down and rest on the
    earth
that mates with them and they sing
songs of prehistoric times
and hymns to the morrow that's
    coming
I have planted my Foundation here
and it shall serve as a rock
for those who farm the future
and defend the flag
carrying on the thrilling traditions
of free enterprise
and the power of wishfulness
the wish I have nurtured all the way
that tomorrow will be better

Aye,
my heart is buried in the rooks and
    rills
the billowing hills and secret trails
of Big Rock Valley

Aye,
and we've replanted
the image of the New Age
frontier in the exotic South

AT BOTH BIG ROCK VALLEY
(Michigan) AND THE E & D CAT-
TLE RANCH (Florida) you will find
replicas of *Edward Lowe's Round
Table*. It is an impressive unit, seat-
ing twelve persons at any one session. It is used to develop new

entrepreneurs, to plan projects, to extend the Cell System, and many related operations. You may find yourself a seat at this exclusive table where Edward Lowe and his peers greet new defenders of independent small business in the free American tradition.

CHALLENGE

*If you happen to believe as I believe
we've got a lot to do
We've got to run at all brick walls
and see our way clear through*

*We challenge the present blockages
in an aggressive God-fearing way
Single the plusses
bare bones with no fusses
head high and determined, we'll say:*

*Hail to our freedom that's slipping
for we're taking a whipping
Our freedom's eroding today!*

P.S. WHAT I BELIEVE

I believe in Don Quixote's mission, I believe the dragons (brick walls) can be demolished.

I BELIEVE WE CAN DO IT!

Has my journey been booked by a senseless guest.

When I needed Don Quixote at his very best?

Must I fight the dragons while victory is pale
or tilt at windmills to no avail?

Has all the good been drunk from the Holy Grail?

Who shall lead us when all others fail?

History tells us that we have a chance.

If we will help raise Quixote's lance.

AND I BELIEVE IN <u>YOU</u>

*Pray for the plight of the
Entrepreneurs
lacking of knowledge, understanding and love.
They are at the mercy of greed
from the nest of the Washington
doves.*

*We must revolt — let our needs
be known!
Remember, have faith, and we
will overcome
the brick walls that we have to
scale;
but don't give in to the bastards
We are not for sale!
HAIL ENTREPRENEUR!*

SECTION FOUR
ON WIT & WISDOM

Dear Reader,

This subject is a difficult one, because sometimes the "witty" isn't witty and the wisdom doesn't seem to be wise. But here's how I figure it: maybe what I think is witty, you may find to be wise. And what I thought was wise, may appear funny to you. So I put it all together in this section. Have fun, will you?

YOUR INDULGENCE, PLEASE

Wisdom, if it comes at all
*   Comes from battles you've*
*   lived through*
Because the only way you can
*   survive*
Is by learning something new

Now the lessons you intend to
*   share may be homely,*
*   may be pretty*
And if they're not very dog-
*   gonned wise*
There's a chance they may be
*   witty*

THE WIT & WISDOM
of a Veteran Entrepreneur
FUNNEL VISION

How to see what should be seen. (The black dot versus the white square)

They asked me what I could see inside the square. "O, I see a black dot," I told them. "With all that *white space*," they scolded me, "And all you can see is that *little black dot!*"

I realized them that I was looking through the wrong end of the funnel. When you look into the large end of the funnel, your outlook is held in a very tight focus, and all you can see is the little black dot through the small end.

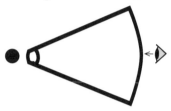

But, if you turn the funnel around and let your vision see *into* the small end and *out* through the large end you will get a much expanded view etc.

Some funnel, eh kid?

Make love and have lots of funnel.

This one had me puzzled for a long time...

Is this glass half-empty or half-full?

The answer is —it all depends?

Is it being filled? *(In which case, it's half-FULL)*, or

Is it being emptied? *(in which case, it's half-EMPTY)*

Life is not a thing, it is a process.

Count your blessings! *(But count-'em right)* 1 plus 1 equals 2. It ain't necessarily so...

Sometimes *(if you're lucky)*

1 plus 1 *(side by side)* equals 11! You can lose 9 points if you count wrong. As a general rule, if two plus two equals three, the person doing the counting wants it to look that way.

There is no such thing as a bad day!

Whether the day brings fog, sleet, blizzard or storm—it does not matter...

Some days are *better* than others (no day is a loser).

Every day that comes your way is your chance to be up to bat, every time you're at bat is your chance to hit a homer.

When you run out of days your ball game is over. Thank God for every day!

Each day is good for you. Try to be good for it.

IS YOUR HEAD IN THE CLOUDS?

It pays to know what business you are in...

■ There once was a barber, who thought he was a haircutter, when actually he was a forensic psychologist.

■ There once was a schoolbus driver, who thought she was a transport worker, when actually she was a baby-sitter.

■ There was a fellow who invented *Kitty Litter,* and thought he was in the pet accessory business, when actually he was in the advertising, promotion and marketing business.

That last one was *me,* and I discovered this truth *(which is as good as discovering Kitty Litter):* Once you know better what you are doing you'll be able to do it better, keep your head in the clouds but stand on solid ground!

Football tickets are not for *you* to see the game. The success-minded entrepreneur uses things of value to build lasting good will for his business.

If a ticket to the game looks good to you, think how good it might look to your banker.

Keep your eye on the big game *(which is the building of your business)*.

Use the tickets to the little games to advance your own team's progress. Success is not a spectator sport.

THINGS I LEARNED ALONG THE WAY

I bought two dozen little chicks once, brought them home, put them in a chicken coop with a wire fence around the lot and by golly, I made a mistake. I didn't take the time to ask the guy if the chickens were roosters or hens, males or females. The roosters breed, the hens lay eggs, and the egg layers are what make your money, unless you butcher them and eat them. But, of the chickens that I purchased, only

one was a hen. The roosters got arguing amongst themselves, the hen was worn out because they were all trying to breed her. If I had only had one or two roosters out of the flock that I got, I would have been much better off. Everyone had a loud mouth and the poor old hen didn't know which way to turn. Organize your flock before you put too much investment in hot shot breeds or big deals. They just wear out your banker.

As a general rule, you can never have a poultry farm, if you start with one egg.

PONDERING

Pondering is not a procedure to be taken lightly. I call it a procedure because it is not a whimsical effort or routine that one indulges in without preparation, considerable thought and planning. It is sort of like going on a picnic—alas for the arranger of such an affair if he purchased the ribs but forgot the matches.

The dictionary gives considerable lineage to the word "ponder". Amongst the dozens or so descriptive words, I picked three that fit my needs to explain my pondering routine: *to mull, muse, speculate.*

I have speculated about pondering, both before or after a good session, and have decided that it is a time that your mind communicated with YOU. Most pondering is done in silence. The language that is used by your mind is probably the one you speak most prevalently. As a general rule, your lips don't move, your gaze may appear to be far adrift, your eyes may be half closed or squinting. Do not confuse pondering with merely thinking. When you ponder, your mind is used with a more in-depth concentrating procedure.

I mentioned that your mind communicates with you. Not **for** you, but **with** you. In my case, my pondering mind is located just above and a bit behind my eyes. It's not at the base of my skull, on top or on either side, but just above my eyes. Don't get the impression that I take thinking lightly. It, of course, reacts much faster than pondering. Thinking is used more in daily routine chores, mathematics, engineering, spelling, talking.

There is a difference in your mind and body and I separate the two into classes of their own. My body is in my chest or torso area, above my midriff. My mind tells it what to do, much by instinct. The less important moves are done by instinct. The more important moves are done by thinking. Those of serious consideration are pondered over. Don't confuse worrying with pondering.

Pondering spots are many and varied. Most pondering is done alone—seldom in a crowd, but in locations, like the park, the beach, or a bench in a museum. There may be many folks around, but basically a person removes himself to seclusion. The atmosphere of location has a bearing on the procedure of pondering. Surely at a crowded cocktail party one would be amiss in trying to sit in the corner to ponder. Think flippantly about the girls, the fellows, the music. or the chatter, yes, but not ponder.

The category of location is important. Accepting the fact that pondering is in-depth thinking, you will naturally wish to ponder things of interest to you and try to construct in your mind that atmosphere that is conducive to what you wish to ponder.

X BILLION DOLLARS

The debt you owe yourself. There's a pernicious philosophy going around these days like a bad cold. Try not to catch it. It goes under a variety of symptoms, spelled like this:

I was promised a rose garden. Life was supposed to be a piece of cake. They told me I had it coming to me.

It can best be summed up under the heading: THE WORLD OWES ME A LIVING. You owe it to yourself to grow out of this delusion.

LETTER TO AUSTIN

Okey-dokey, Austin... I'm ready to admit it. It's true. Yes, your Grandpa Lowe, my grandson Eddie, *has a lot of money.* It's not a secret. The IRS knows it.

In your days to come, it's entirely possible that you might become a person with a lot of money too. So I'm going to tell you a secret that's really not a real secret but it's not widely known, and I'd like you to understand it.

This may surprise you, but for many years, more than a few, your grandpa was already well-off but—guess what?—*he never had any money!*

Here's why: he was always putting the money back into his business. Instead of skimming personal benefits off the top, he steadfastly kept on improving his product. He reinvested. He was building plants, expanding production, augmenting the quality he had created by, in his own words, "making the best better," hiring more people, making the world a better place to live in.

Yes, he kept his family in good stead but he wasn't out buying himself Lear jets or a string of Rolls Royces. He kept his nose to the grindstone. He was dedicated to the welfare of his business. He wasn't ready to let well enough alone and go off and play shuffleboard.

Do you hear me, Austin? Your grandpa wasn't thinking like a millionaire and he didn't live like a millionaire. He doesn't even like the word "millionaire."

I hope that's a lesson for you. You'd be surprised how many successful people don't put on a fancy front. And you'd also be surprised at how many of the flashy ones are putting up a false front, when they are only inches away from possible bankruptcy.

Your grandfather's example should give you a lot to learn from.

Love ya

Grandpa Huber

Are you creative— or what?

HOW TO PAY YOUR DEBT

Today's headlines are busy trying to figure out if the U.S.A. is a "debtor nation" or a "creditor nation." I think a more vital question is one each of us should ask ourself— *"Am I a creditor person or a debtor person?"*

Here's a balance sheet to ponder: God, your parents, your genetic history and the luck of the draw gave you your life. By accepting that gift, *you start off in debt.* You owe it to yourself to do something worthwhile with your life. That's the *only* way you can pay the debt. You've got to make the most of what you've been given. Your obligation is to do your darnedest to fulfill your own potential. You are in debt to yourself. Your life is your chance to pay it off.

Here's an article we ran in our *Main Street Journal.* It's a pretty thorough discussion on what makes you creative. We know the entrepreneur is a creative type—but just because he or she is creative doesn't give anybody a free ride...

"CREATIVITY"

What is it? How to recognize it? Are you a creative person?

What does it mean to be *"creative"?* What *is* creativity? *Who* is creative? Who is *not?* The conventional meaning of the term relates the creative quality to "aesthetics"—the philosophy of taste or perception of what is beautiful. Does "creative" apply mainly to the artists or perhaps a poet? To be regarded as cre-

Look At The Word

ative would it help to lisp a little or wear a beret?

In a general way, to *"create"* means "to form something out of nothing." Specifically it means "to bring into existence". It means "to originate, to begin, or to initiate". It also means to be "imaginative" or "productive".

THE MAIN STREET JOURNAL subscribes to the Edward Lowe theory of the cellular economy ("The Cell System"). Because that theory rests on the platform of a "living economy", attention is directed to *the creative forces within the economy.*

The question to be answered is: can the *entrepreneur* be called creative?

The Real Meaning

In truth, the term "creative" is basically an *economic* word. It derives from the Latin word "creare", meaning "to cause to grow"—to *produce* or *to increase.*

If the economy is to grow, what force will help it grow? What role does creativity play in the development of a nation's economy?

When the characteristics and dimensions of the creative personality are analyzed will this lead us to the recognition of authentic entrepreneurs? If the creative profile is defined will it help those persons who have hitherto felt "uncreative" to stand up and be recognized? Will such a self-recognition encourage prospective entrepreneurs to move ahead and develop their potential capacities?

In this time when the commercial culture tends to thwart and many times to stifle the entrepreneurial spirit, a survey of the distinctive characteristics of creativity may well be in order.

Why All The Hard Work?

Is creativity an inborn talent or compulsion? Is it related to intelligence as such? Or is it an acquired character trait, a behavioral tendency? Can it be developed in practice? Can it be learned?

How is a person to know if he or she is truly creative?

To begin with, there is an unmistakable trait. If *this* is missing, there is no need for any further examination. *The creative person is invariably a hard worker.* They are hard workers, not because they are forced or bulldozed to work hard, but because their energy level is high and they are *motivated* to use that energy in their pursuits.

Creativity depends on intrinsic motivation. The "will to create" is generated from *within*. The first thing it produces is the *necessity* to create something. (This is why Edward Lowe insists that entrepreneurs are *born*, not made.) To be prodded into action intrinsically means the prod comes from inside, from the inner depths of the personality. This intrinsic motivation *fuels* creativity. No fuel, no flame.

That need to act stokes the furnace which disciplines the creative spirit. It provides the focus of dedication for a project or a goal.

It generates the power to concentrate intensely—to grind away undisturbed for long hours. This "inner fire" stimulates the concern for craft, the involvement with ideas, the resistance to distraction, unattracted to external rewards.

Study these traits. These are the essential marks of the creative spirit and of the entrepreneur as well. These inescapable traits are why such "types" are often called "obsessed".

Now we confront the *key symptom* of the creative-entrepreneurial personality. Creativity depends on attention to *purposes* as much as *results*. "Why" comes before "How."

Problems Are No Problem

Although they find answers, this signifies that creative types are not primarily problem-*solvers* in the mechanical, pragmatic sense. They have a flare for asking the right questions, not just for finding workable answers. Until the question is properly formulated, no answer can be forthcoming. Before a problem can be solved, the **nature** of the problem must be determined. The creative type is a problem-*finder*.

Such minds take a substantial time *pondering* the nature of the problem. *Is* there a problem? *Why* is there a problem? Where did it come from? What will happen if it is solved? Will the cure be worse than the disease? Less creative people take a problem for granted and are geared to search for practical solutions as swiftly as possible.

Creative people do not regard problems as irritations. Nor perplexing. They find problems interesting, even entertaining. If they have a weakness, it is because they cannot resist the challenge of a new intriguing problem that may come along. (This is the only lure that can draw them away from the project they may be currently working on.)

There is a prevailing notion that the entrepreneur is recklessly irresponsible in his appetite for taking risks—like riverboat gamblers with no tomorrow. Nothing could be more misleading.

Irresponsible Gamblers?

As with all creative persons, entrepreneurs stand ready to act responsibly in pursuit of their goals. *Responsibility also means risk.* This doesn't assume a frivolous penchant for gambling. Entrepreneurs are not foolhardy. When they are dedicated to perfecting an innovative project. they will not be stopped or dismayed by obstructions or hazards along the way.

The greatest risk they take, of course, is the risk of failure. In the course of creating what is new and untried, failure is always a possible outcome.

"Status Quo" (which somebody has called, "Greek, for the mess we are in")—to the creative entrepreneur the *Status Quo* is not a fixed inevitability. *It is a target for change.* The creative spirit never lets well enough alone.

This is why such types tend to value and invent new ideas —ideas that are fresh, elegant, powerful and deep. When faced with a material problem, here and immediately now, the creative reflex resorts to the *power of ideas*—the intangible mental blueprints for changing the situation.

Is intelligence involved? Of course. *Creativity* is intelligence—*with a creative accent.*

This explains why the power to create is a property of the mind, more than of the *brain*. The creative power emerges from a number of contributing characteristics. IQ is important, but it is not enough.

Cowards Are Not Creative

It takes more than intellectual competence. Many persons who do superbly in school show little imagination. In fact, the academic environment commonly discourages creative impulses.

I.A. Richards believes that the ordinary person suppresses *9 out of 10* impulses, because he is incapable of managing them without confusion. Says Dr. Richards, "The non-creative person goes about the world in blinders because what he might see would upset him."

This emphasizes another creative quality—*bravery.* The creative entrepreneur is brave enough to deal with his own impulses. He wears no blinders. This is important because in order to respond to originality, one must be able to perceive it.

The creative spirit has courage enough to enter the untracked wilderness of new ideas! That spirit is strong enough to think and to work alone—in creative autonomy, thinking what none so far has dared to think. This self-reliance provides the strength to make decisions.

Every phase of the creative process demands a decision—"Go" or "No-Go". Without the guts to decide, creativity withers on the vine.

The chief distinction of creative courage is the refusal to be "fenced in". This applies especially to the entrepreneur who refuses to fence *himself* in. He has the daring to think and work at the "edge" of competence, never content to "play it safe" within the comfortably established range of experience.

Living On The Edge

The term "Open Mind" is a fitting caption for this type. No field of endeavor, no subject matter is off-limits. The creative person is confident that if the motivation leads him or her into absolutely strange pastures, he will be able to come to grips with it—whatever new techniques or language it involves.

No mountain is too high to climb.

In fact the creative person may find stress outlets in auxiliary creative hobbies. This is why a Winston Churchill took up painting. Creativity is a key to the universe of art, invention and all kinds of self-discovery.

This is why it is a social crime to tolerate conditions that bottle up the creative impulses—especially those in the economic sphere which are so desperately needed today.

These observations on the nature of creativity demonstrate that the power to create is a basic human trait. Not everyone has it, but the *entrepreneur* excels in its exercise.

That's pretty solid thinking, I think, and it says things that needed to be said that haven't been said before. From all of it, we can draw some basic conclusions. *Here are principles of mine:*

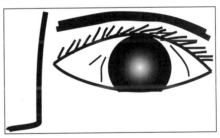

■ You've got a creative eye—keep it open! (*A closed eye misses a lot*)

■ Your mind is a muscle USE IT! (*Minds get flabby without exercise*).

■ Every minute is a coin to spend. (*Which is voided when not used*)

■ Be a WHATIFFER, not a YAH-BUTTER! Spend your energy pushing good ideas into action. Don't make a career out of resisting strange ideas.

■ Give your creative urge a free rein. *(Approach every fact of life: "How can this be better?"*

Following these guidelines will help you pay off your debt to yourself. They will very effectively wipe out the phony notion that the good things of life are free, and that all you've got to do is wait for them to be delivered.

The good life comes to those who earn it.

SOME SPECIAL PONDERING NOTES

Now let's think about what I call the *"Progressive Trinity"*. I see the process of a successful production as going through three phases, pretty much like this:

PHASE ONE—AN IDEA IS BORN

PHASE TWO—THE IDEA IS
        DEVELOPED.

PHASE THREE—THE IDEA IS PUT INTO
        ACTION BY
        IMPLEMENTATION.

Study those stages, one by one:

ONE

A dark closet might be a great place to conceive an idea. Fact is, that conception can occur just about anywhere—in a speeding car or in a tourist seat on the Concord en route to Paris, France. These are all opportune places to connect with an exciting idea in the world of sales, innovation and financial independence.

BUT YOU MUST BEWARE— YOU EAGER ENTREPRENEUR!

Your idea is just scratching the surface of reality. It has just barely got off the launching pad. Now the fuse has to be lighted and the course has to be controlled. I can illustrate this in some of the well-known inventions of the past century.

Think of any of them—the internal combustion engine, Eli Whitney's cotton gin, the Wright Brothers airplane, Henry Ford and assembly line production, the Apple computer, Velcro, Scotch tape, cat box filler *(Edward Lowe's KITTY LITTER)*. Each break-through product initiated a whole new industry. *INITIATION is the cradle for all such products.*

They each started with an idea—a conception of a new way (tool, method or product) to meet a need—such a cottonpicking, flying, speeding up manufacturing and calculations for taking care of pets.

TWO

The old saying has it that "Nothing is so powerful as an idea whose *time has come.*" The problem is that the time does **not** come until the idea takes on some flesh and blood. Depending on the nature of the idea, this means blue-printing, tool dyes, sources of raw material, cost projections, plans for distribution, etc., etc. In the case of my *KITTY LITTER* I had to work out packaging, pricing, brand-naming, processing, and marketing outlets all at once.

This is the DEVELOPMENT stage, where you take the baby out of the crib and try to teach it how to walk. Too many (maybe 90%) of ideas never get out of the "Innovation" stage. Those that undergo constructive development have got a good chance of "learning to fly"—but only if they get into Stage Three which is IMPLEMENTA-TION.

THREE

Can I give you a football analogy about this "PROGRESSIVE TRINI-TY"? *Stage One* would be the "Blackboard Session" where the coaches explain the new play to the team, chalking the diagram on the board. *Stage Two* comes when the game is in progress and the quarter-back calls the new play. This is a passing play and when the quarter-back releases the ball the plan has been developed. If and when the end catches that pass and manages to run with the ball the whole process is finally in the stage of *implementation.*

This stage for the entrepreneur is where operating capital is funded, personnel are hired, and a sales team takes the developed product to market.

How many times the ball gets dropped between Stage Two and Three! It reminds me of the ancient verse, *"For want of a nail the shoe was lost—For want of a shoe the horse was lost—and for want of a horse, the rider was lost."* That explains what "The Progressive Trinity" means to me. It all starts with INNOVATION—where the idea is born. Without an idea there can't be any action at all. But it takes DEVELOPMENT to get that baby up on its feet. And it takes IMPLEMEN-TATION to get it running in the right direction.

For want of implementation, the development is lost. For want of development, the idea is lost. So, as I told you: *Entrepreneurs—beware!*

Do you want
to join
a club?

CLUBS I BELONG TO, AND PERHAPS YOU SHOULD ALSO BELONG?

Membership in each club requires the Scout Pledge.

© 1993

I WORK MY ASS OFF

Some persnickety folks would prefer to call this association a club for *"People Who Work Their Fingers To The Bone"*, but, believe me, IWMAO is more easily and honestly understood by just about everybody.

For entrepreneurs especially, the standard of "Hard Work, Enthusiastically Rendered" is the bottom line for success. Success just doesn't happen for the half-hearted, the take-it-easy and the shiftless crowd.

If you want a running start for success (which is what it takes) then begin by giving every task the full measure of your effort.

IWMAO is right on target. You will wear your badge with pride.

THE NATIONAL ASSOCIATION FOR THE ADVANCEMENT OF PERSONAL PRIDE

It takes pride to stand out in the crowd. To be proud of yourself personally requires you to be worthy of that feeling.

This club appeals to everybody by saying, "If it doesn't make you proud, don't do it!" And it has a little anthem,

Act proud and true
Be proud to be you!
Look'em all in the eye
Hold your head up high!

Self-pride will make better citizens of us all. It will help us be loving grandparents to the needful young and helpful children to the dependent old.

It will help every ethnic category and individual to look into the mirror and ask, *"Why am I not liked?"*

THE GOLDEN RULE CLUB

Do Unto others As You Would Have Them Do Unto You

The Golden Rule has been the highest standard for every culture in the known history of man. It unites all religions and all ethical beliefs.

Our Club asks its members to keep the "Rule" in mind—practice it wherever and whenever possible. Try it in practice and see how it makes life better for all concerned. Saint John's last words were, "Little children, love one another."

In our terms, the club says, "Treat your neighbor as you would like to be treated."

Isn't it time for mankind to join up with the human race? © 1993.

THE GREEN HAT BRIGADE

Safety and hygiene are your own responsibility.

Inspect your own Space!
Keep your house in order!

Green Hard Hat
The green hat system of progress is a *"must"*

THE MILLIONAIRE'S CLUB

The Buck Starts Here! Your first million dollars starts with the first buck.

Face facts: form your own club to advocate rules of internal understanding and encourage high morale.

AS A GENERAL RULE

(Excerpts from the Edward Lowe Encyclopedia of "General Rules" which compresses a lot of wisdom into every little space.)

#1, AS A GENERAL RULE, THE NUMBER "1" WILL START AT THE BEGINNING OF THE COUNT.

This is a general rule that can be taken several different ways. In the case of a fighter, #1 starts at the time that he knocks his opponent down and waits for #10, which means he has won the bout. In the case of buying flowers in Holland, the count begins at a large number and works down. In other words, if you are going to buy roses in Holland, they will start them out at so much per dozen. The clock will start depleting itself from 15 to 14 to 13 to 12 and so on, and you try to time it so that you can buy the roses at the cheapest price. As far as I'm concerned, it would be a business expression, that you start at #1 and work up until you are successful.

#2, AS A GENERAL RULE, NEVER CALL TIME OUT WHEN YOU'RE WINNING.

I always figured that in business, winning is a momentum and once you stop that momentum from growing, or at least holding, you don't want to call time out. The minute that you call time out when you're winning, is when the competitor will sneak in and then you won't be the winner, you will come in second place.

#3, AS A GENERAL RULE, HANDS-ON MANAGEMENT IS BETTER THAN HANDS-OFF MANAGEMENT.

Hands-off management is what I classify as absentee management. They found out that in the franchise business, the person that had part ownership in any franchise, whether it's fast-food, mowing lawns, cleaning septic tanks or whatever, if the person that ran that franchise had a partial interest in it, it would have a better chance of being a success. And, although the main owner of the franchise might be absent, the part-owner of the franchise would be there and watching the store.

#4, AS A GENERAL RULE, IF THOSE WHO WORK FOR YOU AREN'T DOING THEIR JOB, THEN IT APPEARS TO OTHERS THAT YOU AREN'T DOING YOURS.

It's a big responsibility to guide people in their working arrangement in a business so that it is advantageous to the owner as far as profits are concerned. And, believe me, you have to do your job as the owner of the business. If you think you're a hot shot to the point that you think you can go out and play golf, or you can go down to the bar or horsing around doing something else, other people will know what you are doing. The fact is, they probably know more about what you are doing than what you think they know. And then, your business will start falling apart because the people that work for you won't think that you know what you're doing. And by golly, I don't think you do, either!

#5, AS A GENERAL RULE, THE DEPTH OF THE WATER IS JUDGED BY HOW DEEP THE BOTTOM IS, NOT HOW HIGH THE SURFACE IS.

The question then is, how deep is the water? The answer, just six inches above being able to drown. When you get into a business deal, you better make sure that you can keep your head above water by hook or by crook. You can drown in a pool that is one inch above your nose, and it doesn't make any difference whether the pool is 50 feet deep or whether you're lying down in one foot of water. Anyone that can swim can do it in deep water— but what happens if you get a (money) cramp you didn't expect?

#6, AS A GENERAL RULE, IF YOU TELL SOMEONE WHAT TO DO, YOU'RE INTERFERING.

I've found so many times that to be a know-it-all is to always be telling someone what to do.

Sometimes you have to give the person that you are directing the opportunity to have their voice in the way that something should be done. After all, who knows, they might know more about that than you think they know, or that they DO know. In that case, you are probably interfering with them and if this happens repeatedly, it would probably develop a knot in their stomach that would not be good for good business practices or your stomach either. Cramps are deadly in sports and business.

#7, AS A GENERAL RULE, RESEARCH IS NO BETTER THAN THE ONE WHO HEADS THE RESEARCH.

If you want to do research in your business, you have to know what you want to do, what your goal is, and where you wish to end up in the research procedure. If the person doesn't know a few simple facts such as that, then the research that is performed in that project will not be done properly or have a result that is what you wished for.

#8, AS A GENERAL RULE, DON'T FALL IN LOVE WITH YOUR ASSETS.

And, I might add with that, don't dance with skeletons. This is not an original general rule with me, I learned this from a fellow down in Tennessee who had a charcoal company. I asked him why he was selling a division of his company and he said, "Well, it was time that I sold it because I got a very good price." He said, "I like the business, but I didn't fall in love with it so it made it

easier for me to depose of it when the time was right." Then he added, "Also, don't dance with skeletons. If there is something that you have become involved with and it's not going right, if you're not making money, if it's giving you a fit, if it's giving you a knot in your stomach, it really is a skeleton and you should get rid of it. Either bail out, sell it for whatever you can get out of it, but don't dance with skeletons. It ain't fun."

#9, AS A GENERAL RULE, IT IS EASIER TO WALK THAN TO JUMP, UNLESS YOU'RE A KANGAROO.

How many people have you seen that try to bluff their way through, try to transform knowledge to others that they know nothing about. Kangaroos have a very odd way to travel, but don't try to compete with them unless you're a kangaroo. P.S. Mother Kangaroos give a lot of free rides.

#10, AS A GENERAL RULE, FISH WITH BIG MOUTHS SWALLOW BIGGER FALSE BAIT.

I've seen so many times a person with a talkative nature actually eat their way into a deal that is not proper because of their big mouths. And, if while being offered the bait that is false, you are so busy listening to your mouth rattle off, you'll finally take the bait, then get taken to the pea patch.

#11, AS A GENERAL RULE, IF WE'RE NOT WILLING TO MAKE MISTAKES, WE WON'T BUILD ANY SUCCESSES EITHER.

I have put many, many miles on

a car; I have put many, many miles in the air, I have spent untold amounts of money in ventures that I knew not what the answer or the outcome would be. I have lost many, many dollars in ventures that were not destined to be successful. But, also if I had sat on the front porch in a rocking chair, every morning to every night, without making the decision, I would not be where I am today. I don't know what the figures are, but they say that if 30% of your deals are successful, even 20% are successful, you will come out alright because one of them might be a big enough deal to make up for all the slack on the other deals. A way out of this particular general rule is that if you go back to general rule #8, don't fall in love with your assets and don't dance with skeletons, you can get out of those deals fast so that the mistakes that you make are not a rope around your neck to drown you in eaten-up capital.

#12, AS A GENERAL RULE, THE TENDENCY TO PROCRASTINATE TAKES PRECEDENT OVER THE TENDENCY TO MOTIVATE.

My, oh my, isn't it easy to say I'll do that tomorrow? Or, no I won't call this fellow today, I'll talk to him later. Or, how many people in the stock market have said let's wait and see if the prices go down before I buy, or if the prices go up before I sell. Procrastination and motivation go hand-in-hand, but I would be more apt to take the hand of moti-vation and skip to the loo, than to take the hand of the procrastinator and be a fool in slow death.

#13, AS A GENERAL RULE, A BIG DEAL ISN'T A BIG DEAL UNLESS IT'S A BIG DEAL.

#13 is one of my famous, or one of my finest, I think, general rules. And, I repeat it more than any other general rule that I have made. Another way of saying that is that a big deal isn't a big deal *until* it's a big deal. I've been through so many business transactions that everyone is satisfied that it's a business proposition that is ready to go through and suddenly someone stalls. Or you can even get the check and when you go to cash it, your big deal crumbles. Don't think that a big deal is a big deal until the check passes the bank and you've got your money in your pocket. Many a gal, many a guy has been left at the altar because someone promised that they would marry them. There are more bridesmaids at a wedding than brides.

#14, AS A GENERAL RULE, THOSE WHO ARE UNDERSTANDING ARE UNDERSTOOD.

If a person is understanding, as a general rule, they listen more than they talk and sometimes silence is golden. And, an understanding person through expressions, through a clap on the back, through a squeeze of the hand, a smile or a look of gratitude, are all indications that they understand. And then of course, they are understood. Who knows, they could become a friend.

#15, AS A GENERAL RULE, THOSE WHO EXPOUND GENERAL RULES DO NOT FOLLOW GENERAL RULES.

You've got to have a little imagination to get around that one. I think that sometimes philosophers, professors in the academic world will expound a lot on what they think, but I don't know as a general rule, whether they really believe it.

So they probably don't follow their general rules in teaching, or as they kind of say, do as I say, not as I do.

#16, AS A GENERAL RULE, THE GAS MILEAGE CAN ONLY BE PROVEN IN A CAR THAT'S SOLD.

Who knows what a car will do on the road unless the owner can take it out and drive it under the circumstances that he feels or wants the car to perform. He has to have patience in learning how to operate the car and it can only be proven after the car is sold. There are all different types of people that run businesses that are looking for margins of profit. Until the business has proven itself at the bottom line, it will be a mystery as to whether or not that dog will hunt.

#17, AS A GENERAL RULE, ADVERTISING IS MERELY A REMINDER. THE SALE IS THE ISSUE.

I have seen so many ads on items that proclaim the benefits of a product, that give the price of the product, give elaborate demonstrations on how it is to be used, and you go out and try to find it and you can't find the product to buy. The sale is the issue. There has never been a product that has been successful with no matter how much advertising, if that product is not on the shelf and made available to the purchaser. Double check your business plan on this one.

#18, AS A GENERAL RULE, A FLAT TIRE SURE SLOWS DOWN THE OTHER THREE.

How many times have you been with a group that is enthusiastic, wants to move ahead, and some dud pulls in and deflates your ego, deflates your enthusiasm, makes everything look like it's bad. No matter how powerful the engine, no matter how much gas you have or what octane, boy a flat tire can sure put the skeebooze on success. Four tires with 32 pounds of pressure make for a smooth ride.

#19, AS A GENERAL RULE, PENNY ANTE IS FUN, BUT GAINS VERY LITTLE, EVEN IN LOSSES.

Many people like to get in the game, but they don't want to take the opportunity of the risk. I had a fellow that I met one time and I asked him what he did and he said that he sold diamonds. I asked him if he sold a lot of them and he said "No, not a lot of them, but three or four good diamonds can make me happy for a whole year". I don't know, he was well-to-do, but he was selling diamonds that were up in the 40-20,000 range and he'd never make it if he was playing penny ante with copper coins. A diamond in the rough is better than no diamond at all.

#20, AS A GENERAL RULE, IF ALL THE PLAYERS KNOW THE PLAY, THEY HAVE A BETTER CHANCE TO WIN THE GAME.

I remember once when a coach sent in a new quarterback with a play. The quarterback first of course called the signals. He saw a fellow open way down on the end, threw the pass, the receiver caught it and made a touchdown. Everyone stood up and cheered and hugged the new quarterback, but the coach pulled him and said "You're benched. The only reason that you made that score was through luck and it wasn't a team play. We don't operate this squad on the chance that we're going to win or that a play is going to be successful. We operate on the theory that everyone knows what's going on so if there's a mistake, we can all take the blame. But also, which is more important, we share in knowing we all were part of the business decision."

#21, AS A GENERAL RULE, ONE GOAL DOES NOT MAKE A SUCCESSFUL SEASON.

Just because you go out the first day out on the road and you score a good sale, don't take a long lunch break, don't have a martini to cele-brate, but get out there and hit that road all the harder. One sale does not make for a successful business. The ratios until you are established, are rather tough. You do 15 or 20 successful business transactions and then you can take the time to set back on your laurels, but always in the back of your mind keep figuring how you can make another success in your sale or in your operation. Review the move so you will improve.

#22, AS A GENERAL RULE, IF YOU ARE NOT DOING SOMETHING, YOU ARE NOT DOING ANYTHING.

"Something" is a vague word. Look it up in the dictionary. Something. What is that? Oh, it's something. Did you have a good sale? Oh, yeah, something happened today. Something this and something that. As a general rule, if you are not doing something, you are not doing much. As a general rule, I would rather say that I am doing a project that I have designed and I know that it's going to be a success. If you are only doing "something," I won't bet on you to win the race.

#23, AS A GENERAL RULE, TOO MANY ROOSTERS WEAR OUT THE HENS.

The Edward Lowe Free Enterprise Theatre Presents:

"What's A Leader?"

A VIDEO SKIT

     Edward Lowe is seated before an oversized chess-board (perhaps drawn on cardboard) in any setting (picturesque) he prescribes—perhaps in the 8-inch "Patio Pool". He is wearing a three-corner Geo. Washington hat, and at opening he is bent over closely studying the chess board on which a bunch of toy soldiers are all lying around in a pile.

OFFSCREEN *(Darlene's voice calls out: Follow the leader!)*

E.L. *(Looks up into camera, cocks hand to ear)*

Hear that? Hey, now *Follow the Leader* is quite a challenge, isn't it? The problem is, if you're about to follow the leader, you sure need to know how you can tell *who* the leader is.

(E.L. points skyward)

You've seen a flock of ducks flying in V-formation, right? Well, that duck at the head of the formation, *that's* the leader.

He's the *point* of the formation. If he ever happens to get shot or struck by lightning or changes his mind and says to heck with being a leader, that whole formation will fall apart—until or unless a substitute leader moves up to take over—which is usually the case. (He looks up again) Most of those ducks are pretty good followers, but to be a good follower you sure got to have a *leader.* Remember that: No leader, no formation.

(Close-up of chessboard, where now one soldier is standing up.)

E.L. If status quo means the mess we are in at this moment, the leader is the first to stand up and say, "Hey! *This can be changed!"* The status quo is no way to go—as far as the leader is concerned.

(Cut Close-Up to board where soldiers are now arranged in V-Formation behind leader.)

E.L. Our leader is not afraid of change. You know why? Because he is in *charge* of *change.* He declares war on the status quo or the way things are, and he *creates* a change.

(He picks up binoculars and looks through them.)

The leader has the guts to look ahead. He's the one who can visualize the future. Because he has a clear picture of the future, he can pass on the inspiration to his followers.

(Cut to chess board, where Ed moves the leader ahead, and in a quick cut, the body of soldiers follows the leader.)

E.L. You can always recognize the leader because he's at the head of the parade—not a the tail end. He's always in motion, always moving ahead.

(E.L. holds up lettered cards, "TRAILBLAZER" etc.) That's why we've always called the leader such things as "Trail Blazer", "Ram Rod" and "Pace Setter." The leader sets the goal. The leader sets the pace toward that goal. In a business plan, it's called "The Mission."

(Close-up of soldier Leader now standing in a flower pot full of mud.)

E.L. The leader is *never* a stick-in-the-mud. He's not a bottom-liner waiting to see what the trend will be, or which way the parade is going.

(E.L. lifts soldier from mud.)

He is a *top-liner,* It's his example which helps organize the parade behind him.

(Close-up of E.L. looking into camera.)

How about you? Are you a leader? Do you want to be a leader? The first requirement is the *desire* to be one. Let me give you a couple of examples to test yourself with... First off, let's say you're stuck in a elevator between floors in a high rise building. There are about six people in there with you. You're really jammed between floors. All right, are you the guy who goes to sleep in the corner, waiting for help to come? Or do you check the controls, the intercom and the escape hatch, looking around for answers to the dilemma? Are you the person who starts to pound hysterically on the door, yelling? Or do you calmly remind the group that building maintenance is quite aware that this elevator is stalled and that rescue will soon arrive?

(E.L. puts on straw hat)

Another example: Let's say you're at a picnic when a sudden summer storm blows up. Do you run for cover to keep yourself dry, and to heck with the women and children? Do you cuss and cry and wonder why the good Lord has let your picnic be rained on? Or do you take care to see that the old folks and the kids are guided to the nearest shelter, which is not a magnet for any lightning bolt?

(E.L. holds up a map of the U.S.)

E.L. Some bright people have come to the conclusion that this country of ours and its business system are OVER-MANAGED and UNDER-LED! I'm not knocking all managers, but I am saying that we are doggonned *short* of leadership. *Where are the leaders?*

(Darlene's voice off-camera) Follow the Leader!

E.L. *(Waving to voice)* OK. The leader knows *what* the game is all about. He knows *why* we are playing the game. He knows *how* to win the game. He's not afraid to stand up...

(Cut to chess board where leader stands ahead of the V-Formation.)

E.L. It has been well-said that if you're not the lead dog, the scenery never changes. I'll let you figure that one out.

(Ed stands to hold up Old Glory)

Here is how you tell if you've *personally* got leadership potential. Do you stand up when the flag is passing by? Are you the *first* to stand up? Do you have a distaste for confusion, and inactivity, and lack of initiative?

(He points to chess board where now toy soldiers are back in disarray.)

Do you have an incurable itch to change the situation to make things better?

(Quick cut: toy soldiers back in formation behind leader.)

(Close-up E.L.)

As Kipling said, "If you can keep your head when all about you are losing theirs and blaming it on you... *then* you are a leader!"

(He salutes flag)

We need leaders. *America needs you!*

FADE OUT

AN ODE TO GRANDMA HUBER

When the stand of trees
Have shed their leaves
And the nuts have all
Been gathered.

When we know the cellar's
Potato bins piled high in
Musty corner.

Then the onions, squash and
Cabbage rank will fill
Winter's edge with flavor.

We know that spring will
Come, rebound with a
Feeling of Love thy neighbor.

The sun will rise in
Flawless skies on the coming
Year's another.

To steadfast pledge to
The Golden Rule and
Love each other's brother.

—E. L.

MORE ABOUT THE QUESTION: "WHAT BUSINESS AM I IN?"

A few notes on the word "MIS-SION", a word that relates to a very important issue, as to what business a person is in. That is, of course, if it has been established that the individual wishes to be his own boss, managing and leading the group of employees that will make the owner and establishment successful.

Example # 1: If a person is engaged in establishing a compound for homeless animals, a dog pound as such, "Mission" might be to care and engage in feeding and providing housing of homeless pets for their protection, housing, and comfort.

But if in the same breath we say, as *Example #2,* one is in the business of manufacturing pet foods or, as *Example #3,* one chooses the profession of studying to become a doctor, both have stated their mission but much more has to be taken into consideration than *Example #1*.

Does the individual in *Example #2* choose dogs, cats, laboratory species such as mice, etc.? Does he choose his method of goals to manufacture—wet canned—dry canned —high quality with nutritional value, or treats and gourmet foods which means selecting limited markets? In the case of *Example #3,* the profession of being a doctor covers a multitude of categories. General

practitioners are rare and hard to find. A brain surgeon is not in the same class as a person prescribing glasses or hearing aids.

In going back in history and answering the question. "What business am I in?", I believe at this point in time I might change my answer and give more careful thought to the important inquiry, "What business are you in?" The question might have been, "What business do you *wish* to be in?" and then approach that goal with a logical and step-by-step procedure as to how to get there.

I proclaimed at the time that I was in the pet supply business, then switched to being in the mining business. That seemed logical to me at the time, but I really believe I was destined to be in the care of pets. Kitty Litter and Tidy Cat were designed for the purpose of cat box sanitation. I purchased the PetPac bird seed business and manufactured seed bells for wild birds; built and established a pet shop in South Bend, Indiana called "Mr. Friendly Pet Shop"; purchased a dog treat company in California (GroKote) which produced dog and cat treats. I developed a full line of catnip toys plus scratching posts and a home catalog for the purchase of gifts through mail order.

During this time I became diverted in my methods. A herd of Angus cattle was developed, intermingled with raising horses. I dispersed the herd in 1976 and then went to auction school and established The Executive Auction Company. In 1972 I purchased the town of Jones, Michigan and discontinued that venture in 1975.

Then I developed an Industrial Park in Cassopolis. Big Rock Valley was in the process of sprouting which now is the base for the Edward Lowe Foundation and the Information Center for privately held businesses. In 1991 I sold the main life line of mining and distributing Kitty Litter and many more projects. We started and stopped. Was it wrong? If so, how wrong? Where would the overall picture be if all had gone right? The better question was why did those other ventures go wrong? Simple Answer: LACK OF PROPER FORESIGHT AND WEAK MANAGERS FOR PROGRESS. I wish I had taken the question: *"What business am I in?"* more seriously.

SECTION FIVE
TOMORROW IS FOREVER

Dear Reader, (especially younger readers):

It used to be said that **"Tomorrow never comes."** This was literally true, because once Tomorrow does arrive, it turns into "Today".

In a deeper sense, however, Tomorrow finally comes, and when it comes, it is **forever.**

You can understand why an older fellow like myself would think this way, I am sure. But my counsel to the younger generations is: **Keep Tomorrow in mind.** It's a good time right now to consider why are you here, what you are doing, and what you will leave behind.

Edward Lowe

END OF THE ROAD

The end of the
Road
Begins here.

The hump of life
Is strained by old
Age and youth.

I would rather be
Remembered when
I'm gone than known
While I'm here.

*L*etter to Austin

I've got a hundred and twenty-five years' advantage on you, young fella, so I hope you will pay me some mind. The question is:

Tomorrow is waiting for you to catch up with it. How are you going to do it?

I ask myself: how can the young people of today be taught the important part they've got to play in the future?

It's not an easy deal. The window of life's opportunity seems to get more complicated as it narrows. There seems to be less and less understanding; more and more confusion about the mission and what it calls for. I'll ask you to remember Mr. Kipling's fine message, "To keep your head when all about are losing theirs and blaming it on you."

To keep progress progressing calls for two mighty big actions—communication and understanding. Austin, those are two ends of the same stick! If it can't be *heard*, there's no sense in *telling* it. Today, in your time, my great-grandson, a whole new language is being forced on you. It's time you learned the language of the computers.

Seemingly simple things have become so complex that many of your generation are being passed up and left behind. Things are moving so doggonned fast the old A-B-C's can't keep pace.

You've got to be growth-oriented. Be ready to replace the leftover relics of bygone times—those of slow knowledge. The range of possibility is as wide as the horizon. It includes doctoring (health), politicking (citizen's security), business systems (manufacturing and commerce), law and order (crime), schooling (children) and maintenance of our home (the earth). Hey laddie—that's a pretty full agenda waiting on you and your kind!

The biggest freedom available to us—in fact, the *most important* freedom demanding our use of it is the *freedom of change.*

You see it all around you—in dress style, automobile styling, engineering, building dressing—even in toys and office equipment. Ask yourself: why hasn't business procedure changed at the same pace? Why are we lagging behind? What's holding us back?

Don't be afraid to keep up with *change.* Encourage your lazy brain to learn the new language (and more are on the way). Push the button that will release the power of your mind. Our manufacturing and administrative procedures have all been speeded up by one giant factor: AUTOMATION.

Just remember this: the mind of man invented automation, data-processing and the computer in all its guises. That means that *your* mind can handle it.

Think of it this way—Tomorrow is a fast train roaring down the track. I'm sorry, but it ain't going to stop to let the conductor welcome you, saying "All aboard, please!" To get on board Tomorrow, boy, you've got to start running right now. Fast as you can, Austin! You've got the power. You've got the potential. You've got me and your Grandpa and your parents pushing you, wishing you well and praying for you.

Tomorrow is counting on you.

Loveya

Grandpa Huber

I WANT TO BE IMMORTAL, TOO!

A club you may want to join

The dictionary told me this much: "Mortality"—the nature of man, meaning that eventually all men must die. "Immortality"—that which lives or lasts forever, being long remembered, having lasting fame.

The great Pharaohs of Egypt, the Caesars of Rome and the rulers of ancient China all went to great lengths to insure their own immortal condition. Mostly they did this with fancy tombs and buried treasures, a Sphinx or a Pyramid and a lot of statues.

In modern times, the honors of immortality seem to go to those connected with the arts and sciences, teaching, politics and executive ability.

Who really deserves having his or her name engraved in this *"Hall of Immortal Fame"*?

In terms of historical achievement, we have quite a list of figures who insured their immortality with great effort on their part. I'm thinking of Moses, Jesus Christ, Noah, Columbus, George Washington and others. You can easily assemble your own list. If we were to review the roster from the beginning of recorded history to current times, the list would be quite lengthy.

I would like to see a roster developed that would feature classical start-up entrepreneurs drawn from the world of business enterprise. My shining example might be Henry Ford. It wouldn't be restricted to Americans, but I am confident there would be a good number of Americans to make it.

Nominees to this list would be proven champions of the free enterprise system, dedicated to initiative, innovation and independence. Those who deserve to be on it must have left their enduring mark of accomplishment in the real world. Their energy should have improved the system, developed the products and procedures and benefited the people as a whole.

I would call this *"The Roster of Immortal Fame for Entrepreneurs."*

As you read that title, I want you to think, *"I, too, can be immortal."* I write these words hoping that some young Upward Achievers are reading it now. I don't refer to those who are content to spend their lives waiting for the fifteenth Vice President to retire so they can qualify for their generous pension with a giant corporation. I refer to those youngsters who are just aching to bust out all on their own, ready to swim on their own power in their own pool, drawn ahead by the magnetism of their private dreams.

Sure, a lot of oldsters are reading this, too, which is fine by me. I hope when they read it a couple of times they will give it to their nieces and nephews... or the kid who delivers their groceries.

The question I want every reader to ask is this: *Is immortality within the reach of the small independent businessman (or woman)* who has made a mark while alive as a member of the entrepreneur set?

I sincerely think so. I think the roster should be started. Perhaps it starts with a club, **"I want to be immortal, too."** I want to be a member. I think I deserve it. How many of you think you should be on that roster with me? I have taken the stand that is wellknown within the small range of my acquaintances:

■ Lowe's will not be sold.

■ Lowe's will strive for growth.

■ Lowe's will go on forever.

■ Lowe's will be a billion dollar company.

It's not vanity that makes me declare this pledge. It comes with the territory. It's a pledge that reaches far ahead of me into the future. It is built into the Great American Dream.

I believe in the dream. I believe in the promise. My dream made me do it.

SAY "HELLO" TO THE FUTURE!

Just a few days ago, I had the privilege of being introduced to the future—and it was free. Not only was I introduced, but I was taken up and engulfed in years to come. It seemed like a dozen Tomorrows. Do you want to be there? Go to Chicago and fly United. Believe me, this is not a commercial pitch. It is just that the entire complex arrival and departure areas are fantastic. Prior to this encounter my #1 terminal was Tampa. It is now #2. The United complex at O'Hare is so futuristic it would make Buck Rogers look oldfashioned.

I mention this drastic design as something that has to be contended with. Whether you personally like it, it makes little difference. Futuristic blowing designs are on the move and engulfing the gullible at a more rapid pace than we wish to admit. Visit Boston, Pittsburgh, Dallas, even Grand Rapids or Decorah, Iowa.

The freedom of change is with us in dress style, automotive equipment, in home building, even toys and office equipment. The question—why doesn't business procedure change? Why are we lagging behind, afraid to do it differently?

Do not get me wrong. I know and you know, the reason most companies are in business—it is for profits. A profit and loss statement is really very simple. Selling Price minus Cost = Profit. The instant the process of manufacturing and sales take over, the word "encumbered" takes effect. The manufacturing procedures and the accounting systems are in effect. How it has changed over the years! Two things were thrown in the pot: the posting machine for the office and powered tool lathes for manufacturing, in both cases—AUTOMATION.

The procedures in both cases grew at a slow but a rapid pace. Slow because many fought the system. Rapid because those who were progressive took the chance and became part of the bulldozer growth pattern of our great country. If it did not do the job, move on, change, review, change plans, innovate, grow. In my first book, *"The Man Who Discovered The Golden Cat"*, on page 121 is a picture of super secretary, Mrs. Egmer—note the old crank telephone on her desk. If you could see in the back room, you'd notice a #14 scoop shovel I loaded the truck with in 1 hr. 20 min. Today we would have a front-end load a Bobcat at best, loading time 18 minutes.

Machine tools and processes are done by computer and the data processing and order complexes are so advanced: the invoice is in the mail at loading time, the cash is in float drawing interest, and margins are calculated in a twinkling.

So what am I whining about?

Only because the system of advancement in mechanical procedures seem to surface, but the real base that was established years ago remains the same. To be perfectly frank, it seems to have dropped back a notch or 10.

COMPUTER FUTURE

The window of life's completion seems to become more complicated as it narrows, and there are less and less understanding people *in my partnership* of completing the plan. The plan as I envision it, revolves around the mission. The extended parts of importance of the mission contain a critical implementation clause, that *it will go on forever.*

The extension of progress revolves and is motivated by *two* very important factors—*communication and understanding.* The understanding bubble to which each of us is confined, is not surface-orientated. *Surface depositions,* if taken seriously, bring out easily recognized faults and assets, which then can be dealt with. Unfortunately, the complexity of seemingly simple things of the past has been so departmentalized in such a short period of time that many of us have, and are still being passed up and left behind. (Reference here is the new field of computerization.) A new language is being forced on those people of past knowledge and importance. The available surplus educational pool made up of students, has been taken up by the computerized information services, and at this point, I feel our reserve is dangerously low. I refer here to educated youth who must replace the past ages. How can the ages of the past catch up? How can the youth of today be taught the important part they must play in the future? The answer is *communication-education-implementation* of the findings between the growth-oriented owners, of our time, youth and elders.

THINKING IT OVER...

My time has come... *Edward Lowe*. It is time, the cat in the dog house remarked, that this damn dog find out that I'm cat. The horrid details of my life and strife are readily available to those who wish to indulge in the rather interesting reading of the fame and fables regarding Edward Lowe in the book *"The Man Who Discovered the Golden Cat"*. Most of it is true *fact*. It is all *true*. I did omit several exciting episodes merely because they were so bizarre if told they would be hardput to be believable. So when you notice I have a far-way look in my eye, a slight smirk while in daydreaming pose, I am reliving the untellables.

But let's get on with it. If so then—if I must be so bold and bare my inner thinkings not of today but of the past, the dreams I've had, the dreams that have matured to the present—and with your help plan for the future. Yes, be not afraid, said the skunk to her kits. Follow my advice, that which I have gathered from experience, then form your skunkered circle, put your nose between your paws, then lift your tail and let us spray...

From my late maturity, in 1947, till mid-maturity, my main goal which passed through my simple mind, was to meet each day as it presented itself. The expressions, "up and at'em," "hold for the rest of tomorrow, whatever it may bring" and be "gung ho" whatever that meant... became my slogans. Gradually, ever so gradually, there crept into the routine the fact that maturity, whether late or never, brought a growing responsibility, ever gnawing. This became apparent by signing one, two, or three more paychecks in addition to those that chose to become involved and come aboard the Good Ship Lollipop.

Nothing promised, nothing given, other than a pledge of responsibilities, galore. You will be to work early, work late, and look to the future. Pledge to IWMAO Club*. We have all done that; that is the reason we're here today. Those who faltered are history. So time has passed but unlike the cockroach or the armadillo, things have changed, not only in my personal image, which is physical, but in the planning mode of thought, word and deed, which comes from the mind. The following thoughts were coined some years back when possibly in a frenzy of uncontrollable seal, I stated *"My company will not be sold, my name, Edward Lowe, will go on forever, and we will become a billion dollar company."*

Although through misconceptions, the communities in my life are under the impression that my business compound has been sold... *not so!* Merely the valuable tradenames, Kitty Litter and Tidy Cat. The use of the distribution representatives and the manufacturing facilities were part of the transaction. The brokers were left not only to those who purchased the company, but to myself to use as I wished for future growth to attain the goal of a billion dollar company.

These goals still remain—emblazoned on my shield.

I AM TRYING TO REMEMBER MY OWN FUTURE

It is practically impossible to forget your past. That's because your past is always following you. Your past remembers you forever. Its memories are all around you.

Your *future* is something else.

Since the future hasn't happened yet, how can you *remember* it?

Man—meaning humankind—is the only species, or so it is said, which is conscious of death-to-come. This means holding the belief that one's life, as we know it, is limited—it won't last forever. And that there is something beyond that limitation, or **after** dying.

We do what we do, and we hope when we are done that our lives here on earth will have been worth something lasting. *You want to leave your mark.* When you are gone, you want your future to remember that you existed—and that you did what you did.

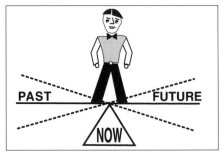

Study that little drawing. If you think of today, this very minute, as *Now.,* and see your time span as a straight line from the Past through Now (the present) to the Future. If Now is a fulcrum, and that line of your development is like a teeter-totter you can visualize how your past and future are closely related.

I know it's easier to think of the future as something unknown, and therefore mysterious, but it's really not.

My personal past has been thoroughly recorded in my book, "The Man Who Discovered The Golden Cat." In writing it, I discovered how vividly the past can be recollected. I think of my life (which has been a good long one) as a record of learning, growing, serving, building and achieving.

That story, as it came back to me, filled in a whole lot of detailing from the past—what I did, how I felt and where I was going. What happened in my boyhood prepared me for the life I led later on.

It has *not* been a lifetime of building up a bankroll or piling up a heap of money. I have never been motivated by the lust for gold. Becoming a millionaire was probably the last of my ambitions. Mostly I did what I had to do, in my time and place.

I had to learn how to earn my own way and how to support my own family. I had to learn the hard way how to build a business within the free enterprise system, and how to keep that business growing.

To do this, I had to learn how to develop a product that served its buyers and kept its quality by improving—*"making the best better"*. Kitty Litter and Tidy Cat did just that.

Once I had built some financial reserves, I was in a position where I could lend a hand to improving my environment. The bulk of my life to that point had been spent in creating my past. (The old truism that *"a man will do what a man has done"* still applies.) My recent years have been devoted to creating a future that will be worth remembering.

When a man spends his lifetime learning things he should be able to share that learning. I didn't have any

trouble in choosing the field I wanted to assist...

I am a self-made entrepreneur. For ten years now I have been developing ways and means to help new generations of entrepreneurs make themselves into growing entities.

The Edward Lowe Foundation was set up as a non-profit philanthropic institution chartered to serve the cause of the entrepreneur. Under its banner we activated the *American Academy of Entrepre - neurs* at our Big Rock Valley compound.

Next, I focussed on the health of the economic environment. That's the soil in which the entrepreneur has to grow. I was a product of the American free enterprise system, and I owed my successful history to the freedom of that system.

But, *hey!* I saw that system cramping up! I saw the interests of small, independently-owned businesses being crippled by oppressive regulations, taxation and other handicaps.

How could my future be remembered if the American opportunity for entrepreneurialism was going to fall apart? This question made me take a wider look at the job to be done. I had to size up all "the brick walls" that were barring our way to a better tomorrow.

I'm telling you all of this because *your* future is *your* business. One of my warnings is to watch out for *"funnel vision"*. A funnel, as you know, has a large opening and a

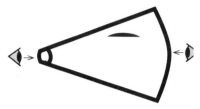

small one. Make sure you're looking out the small opening so you see the *big* picture! It's not enough to go after the "pot of gold" at the foot of the rainbow. You should consider: what's *behind* the pot of gold? *What's behind the rainbow?*

That's where the future is hiding!

THERE'S VERY LITTLE IN MY LIFE I WOULD HAVE DONE DIFFERENTLY.

by Thea Lapham

AN INTERVIEW (Re-printed from BUSINESS INSIGHT, Sept. 1993)

As a child, Ed Lowe peddled newspapers, sold tin cans and killed rats for the bounty their tails would bring.

Several years and one fortune later, Lowe, inventor of Kitty Litter, still relies on street smarts and old-fashioned common sense.

"I'm always working, always plotting and planning," Lowe said. "I have to literally force myself to stop creating, stop inventing, stop envisioning. There are workaholics and thinkaholics. I'm a thinkaholic, I just can't quit thinking, can't quit working."

To prove his point, he conceptualized another Ed Lowe invention based on a drink coaster design.

"There's three things you want to emphasize here," he said. 'There's innovation—which I did just now with this simple plastic disk. Then there's the development and implementation."

"The implementation is the dull part though," Lowe confessed. "I'm like a jack-rabbit: I love the entire start-up process of a business. But once it gets going you'll find me looking for the next challenge."

This self-realization was a crucial step in his business development. Instead of trying to be a square peg in a round hole, he focused on innovating. He hired others to fill the void.

"I've never had a failure." he said. "I always learned **something**. I've had a multitude of failed projects, but never a failure. There's a big difference."

Lowe also owned an auction business, a pet shop and an entire town—Jones, Mich. He owns a glass company in Florida, a sludge reconstituting plant in Green Bay, Wisc., and raises Texas longhorns and black horses at his Florida ranch. He also writes poetry and oversees the Cassopolis-based Edward Lowe Foundation. The foundation, established in 1985, encourages entrepreneurship throughout the United States.

But aging, not amassing fortunes, is Lowe's biggest concern now. "I'm 73-years-old," he said, "so my window of opportunity is getting narrower. I'll be going to the great cat box in the sky soon and that makes me a little impatient. When I talk to someone about doing something aggressive, and they say 'I'll think about it,' I respond by saying 'I don't have time to think about it—at most, I've only got about 10 years left."

"That's why I'm also intolerant of boring people. I like to be around people—until they bore me. I don't like people who talk mediocre stuff. If you're going to talk about something, let's get down to it. Let's cut a deal."

Lowe starts each day at 2:30 a.m., sequestered off with a pen, writing paper and smooth jazz sounds. "I'll do some pre-planning for the day, some reading and general research," he said. "I put the coffee pot on around 4:30 and go back to bed. I wake up again at 5:30 or 6, have some coffee, read the paper or watch the news."

All work and no play can kill entrepreneurial spirit faster than anything though, Lowe said.

"The biggest mistake business people make is forgetting to have fun along the way. If I'm not having fun at what I'm doing, then why do it? It just doesn't make sense. I love my life, I love what I do and it makes me happy. If I make some money along the way, that's great too."

Lowe had his share of personal and professional roadblocks. But, "No matter what, I just keep going. There's no time for stopping and feeling sorry for yourself.

"There's very little in my life I would have done differently," he said. "The key thing to remember is: you can never give up. Just keep driving, keep driving your dream. But if, along the way, you find something wrong with the way your dream is being realized, be ready to make the necessary adjustments."

What happens to my Dreams after my Death?

After Saint Peter has judged the good and the bad.
Isn't there a Hereafter for all the dreams that we had?

THE GREAT AMERICAN DREAM

A bad dream only takes an instant, but when it is happening it seems like forever. That is the case of many, many would-be success stories that end up in failure because the seeker of success became involved in a nightmare that, in many cases, started out on the wrong foot. They were faced with adverse conditions—stumbling blocks and frustrations that were nearly impossible to overcome.

As a general rule those who fail are loners, not by choice but by happenstance. Not only loners fail but also entrepreneurs who are, in most cases, the loneliest lot of the litter. But have heart, oh, entrepreneur, the help is at hand. The system amongst many has been put together, the team who will help is here—we call it THE CELL SYSTEM.

I am proud to know that I have been part of the Great American Dream. My special dream now is to see to it that our *American Academy of Entrepreneurs* makes the Cell System come to life—teaches it, explains it, demonstrates it. And in so doing, helps keep the American Dream an exciting motivator for generations yet to come.

If the dream poops out, America will wither away. I intend to be faithful to my dream. How will I do it?

I am going to keep on dreaming. As a general rule, the dreams of great dreamers are not the same as those who only dream—because one has an action plan and the other is just a dream.

HOW IT SEEMS TO ME

(Some of my thoughts you'll have to work at, if you really want to understand them)

A statement about some fundamental happenings which may possibly stimulate your thoughts. I call it: *THE BIRTH OF GOD.*

At the beginning of time, before the sun was released for glory, an Eternity was chosen within Forever. It was so chosen to establish an endless cycle of instructions directed to the life that was being formed. The souls within this life style would set the pace and function of LOVE. At that particular point, the EOBIONT structure has nothing but the blackness of Forever surrounding it, forming one huge mass of compressed ATOMICAL mystery.

The compression of the mass was so condensed that it could not be penetrated; it was neither solid nor liquid, neither hot nor cold, its total was neither heavy nor weightless; there were no ORGANIC MOLECULES present. It was not important because there was no light.

Buried within this complexity of nothing, tucked away but dormant, was a single BIOPOESIS that had not been given the miraculous gift of REPLICATION. Why or how, is a mystery that will forever remain unanswered, unanswered because there is no answer, such as how to describe time or space.

The mysterious single BIOPOE-SIS was the balance of the mass, undisturbed and dormant because it was undisturbable. It had no reason to be disrupted until the mystery of life energized by the strength of Time gave heed to its capabilities to grow.

With a mere pulse that was so minute that it was nothing, the complacency of time was disturbed and a tremendous expansion came about, so forceful that it formed the two necessities of life, THE SUN, and the miraculous feat of REPLICA-TION.

It is within the bowels of this compressed substance the image of GOD could possibly have been conceived by the HOLY TRINITY.

Like trying to find the end of a path that forms a circle, to travel that path searching for the end would be of no avail if that was the ultimate goal. To become more aware of what the line represents, picture one walking that path with Forever on one side and Space on the other, with both sides giving heed to the complexity of the mysteries of the beginning of Time.

At the moment of conception the explosion of the mass generated the expansion of space. The seed is still traveling billions of times faster in a second than light travels in a year, EON multiplied by forever. It outstrips man's present functional description of the mass. It travels to unexplored expanses, seeking to form new experiences of its own.

Would it be that today, captured in the lowly rock formed by the explosion of conception, there be a glimmer of life in the form of yet another single BIOPOESIS ready to be released by an unknown force to be shot into eternity to be free to build and solve its own destiny, to build and solve its own mysteries? Could be—*why not?*

SOME DEFINITIONS

THE HOLY TRINITY—A three-fold personality existing in the one Divine Being or substance; the union in one God of Father, Son and Holy Spirit as three infinite co-equal and co-eternal Persons. The following terms are used in the scientific nomenclature employed in defining and fixing the ecumenical statement of the doctrine of the Trinity: **essence, hypostasis or person, individuality, generation procession.** There are seven tests which any definition of the Trinity must meet. It must not be moralistic nor unintelligible; it must not be trithestic nor unitarian, it must not be a contradiction in terms nor unhistorical and above all it must not be unscriptural.

BIOPOESIS—The (hypothetical) origination or evolution of living or lifelike structures from lifeless matter.

EOBIONT—A hypothetical chemical structure, supposed to arise during biopoesis, that has certain characteristics of living matter, but is not alive in the fullest sense. Professor W. Pire in Discovery Magazine, August 1935: "A system, which may be eobionts, functions may have been performed by other materials inefficiently no doubt, but well enough to get things started." Eobionts— In 1967; J.D. Bernal King Oreg life, showed that such colloidal bodies could carry on complex reactions and could gradually form what were afterwards referred to as eobionts or pre-vital masses which could carry on a chemical evolution of their own.

REPLICATIVE—The human soul is said to be in a place replicatively, when conceived to be all in the whole, and all in every part thereof.

EON—an age of the universe; an incalculable period one of the longest conceivable divisions of time; a cosmic or geologic cycle; a theological dispensation; an eternity.

HOLY GHOST—The Comforter or Paraclete promised by Christ to abide with and guide His disciples; the Third Person of the Holy Trinity.

WHO WANTS TO BE A 15-MINUTE CELEBRITY?

"I hope I die before I am forgotten"

—*Edward Lowe*

IMMORTALITY...

...Is earned the hard way through:

- *strong faith*
- *good works*
- *supportive friends*
- *and the grace of God*

RULES
OF
INHERITANCE

(1) He who gives while he lives also knows where it goes

(2) Lucky is the one who knows before he goes what neighbors thought of the life he chose

(3) The status quo is no way to go

(4) Every end is a new beginning

SECTION SIX

WHAT OTHERS MAY THINK

Dear Reader,

You may consider this next section as sort of an Appendix. I was reluctant to include it because I didn't want it to look like a personal vanity file. Then I was convinced that the best way to back up my credibility was by including the opinions of people who know me.

After 50 years of being in business, you meet a lot of people. Here are samples of what many folks say about me...

Edward Lowe

"I hope I'm not forgotten before I die..."

—Edward Lowe

Lucky is the one who knows before he goes
What neighbors thought of the life he chose

THE
CANDID
MIRROR
OF
IMMORTALITY

How do you think you'd come out in a survey asking 100 persons, "What do they think of *you?*"

Such a survey should include members of your family, your neighbors (including those you've had difficulties with), old friends, competitors, business associates and a few V.I.P.'s. Edward Lowe's book *"The Man Who Discovered The Golden Cat"* told of his life from *his* point of view. Without any involvement on his part the above survey was conducted to find out what his "community" thought about his life. *Here are a few dozen excerpts.*

Says FRANK WOODS, high school buddy

Ed's down-to-earth way of dealing with people, without being concerned about social status, was another of Ed's unique characteristics.

Woods recalls an instance of this characteristic from when the men were still schoolboys.

"He'd go down and visit the hobo camp. He thought they were interesting and he became acquainted with them." said Woods.

"One day he bumped into one guy and found out the man was going to bed down in an old abandoned stock yard by the railroad. Ed went down there with the old hobo to check out the place to see if it would be alright. When they got there Ed saw that there was nothing for the man to lie down on but the ground. So Ed went and found his friend, Chuck Loupee, whose father had a barn, and he told Chuck that he needed a bale of hay for his hobo friend.

"Chuck wouldn't believe Ed, so Ed had to take Chuck down there and show him his hobo friend," said Woods. "Chuck laughed about that for the rest of his life."

Says ROBERT FOLLETT, retired employee

"He has an aggressive attitude and is willing to work hard to see that his ideas become a reality," said Follett.

"When he thinks of an idea, he doesn't just think about it—he does it," said Follett. "I don't care how wild the idea may be."

"If he has a gut feeling for something, he goes ahead and does it."

As an example of this impetuosity, Follett told of Lowe's visit to Egypt.

"Once Lowe saw a pyramid he wanted to climb it. Lowe was stopped by an official who informed him that visitors were not allowed to climb the pyramids and who then escorted him off. Lowe waited until dark and snuck back over to the pyramid and climbed it. He was promptly arrested by the official, but he **did** climb the pyramid."

Says RICH MUELLER, cousin

"My brother and I have always said that he could've made it in any direction." said Mueller. "If it wouldn't have been Kitty Litter it would have been something else."

"He has a terrific mind and he's constantly thinking of new ideas," said Mueller.

"One of the jobs was loading big, heavy bags of sawdust onto a truck," said Mueller. "We had a guy working for us that was as strong as an ox and Ed said, 'I'll never let that son-of-a-bitch outwork me'."

Mueller's most vivid memories of Lowe come from those days when they worked side by side.

"We talked and joked a lot," said

Mueller. "He was always the first one there in the morning and he was always thinking way down the line. Once he said to me, 'Someday, I'd like to own a whole town.' And he did!"

About 25 years later Lowe bought the town of Jones, Michigan, and turned it into a tourist attraction. That business failed after a couple of years because it didn't draw in enough people, according to Mueller.

"With as many ideas as Ed had, some of them had to fail.," said Mueller.

Says JAMES CRAIN, fellow entrepreneur

"A whole lot of entrepreneurship is courage and financing," explained Crain. "It takes a whole lot of guts to follow an idea through."

According to Crain, these requirements seem to come almost without thought to Lowe, not only in business ventures but in everyday life.

"He's a terribly impulsive person," said Crain. "As soon as he gets an idea in his head, he wants to do it immediately."

Crain mimicked what he describes as a typical Lowe statement, "We're going to Egypt at 12 o'clock tonight, do you want to go?"

"A lot of times he doesn't call in advance to tell you he's coming," said Crain. "You don't know until you look up and see him."

"He's very abrupt," said Crain. "When the fun of the party wears off—boom! He's gone."

"His wives went from one extreme to the other," said Crain. "One thing he did that influenced me a lot was telling me about how flexible his second wife, Darlene, is and how she'll go along with him and give him emotional support instead of always scolding him. They get along very well."

Says DR. FRED MATHEWS, optometrist

"If I was going to come back in another life, I'd want to come back as Ed Lowe," said Dr. Fred L. Mathews, a Dowagiac optometrist and a long time friend of Lowe.

"He has the most interesting life of any person I have ever known," said Mathews. "Not only does he come up with more fresh ideas than anyone I know but he has the resources to pursue the ideas."

"He does things other people only dream of doing. When Ed dreams, he gets up in the morning determined to make it a reality. If it turns out to be a success, great; if not, he doesn't cry about it, he just goes on and does something else.

"His mind is constantly working," said Mathews. "He never shuts down. He'll get up in the middle of the night to jot down notes or even to write poetry if he feels inspired."

Says LYNN DOAN, neighbor

"I think people like you and I would've gave up before he even got started. But Ed believed in his product and pushed it against what most people would have seen as overwhelming odds.

"I give him an A for effort. I have a lot of respect for Ed."

Doan and his wife, Alice have experienced Ed's tenaciousness and how his concern about the future of Cass County brought the men together. Lowe formed a group of men with the objective of devising a plan to improve the county. It was as a member of this group that Doan first witnessed Lowe's leadership ability to set and accomplish goals for the community.

Says RICH WYTMAR, psychologist

Ed likes ideas, he likes to do things. He has this great ability to develop which is related to his love of the land. It's incredible how he can take a piece of property and see different things in it and develop different and various usages for it that are interesting. His love of the land and his ability to do that is analogous to Kitty Litter. He felt this has been his baby and he's had this great love for it and feels that he can do it better than anyone and goes out to develop it as he sees it. I don't think many people recognize that

Ed is an extraordinarily persistent guy. Once he believes in something, just try to talk him out of it. The creativity is really there.

Ed's success story sure as hell can inspire aspiring young entrepreneurs. The basic lesson is if you strongly believe in a direction you must persist in the exploration of all the areas to exploit that idea. The problem with so many areas is that they're given up too early.

Says ED ZAPPA, broker

Ed was truly an entrepreneur from the word go. He had a drive second to none. He was very demanding but he was also very fair. He said that he had the best product in the world, he wanted everybody to know about it, especially the end user, his favorite pet, the cat. When he put that product in his bag and put his name on it, it had to be extra special. He practiced that for all the years that I've known him.

I think his story tells others who want to become entrepreneurs, "Hey I did it, why can't you?" I think it would give somebody reading the book a shot in the arm and would give them a little strength to pursue rather than quit. There's thousands of entrepreneurs coming in with new products and that's the basis of our country. But to get in the grocery business with one item today is very difficult because the costs are so exorbitant.

Says ANNE McELHENEY, distributor

Ed wasn't afraid to take a chance to try anything new. He just went ahead and did it. If it didn't work, he knew right away. He went into something else—some other phase or some other way. When he saw something wasn't working, he didn't hang on. He figured out that was the wrong way to go. You learn that in a hurry. He's very pleasant to everybody. People liked him and I think that was very important.

Says WHIT PALMER, competitor

I think of him as being fierce, intense and extremely competitive. He's not without ego which I think helps to drive the engine. I don't think its a destructive kind of ego. Ego builds a lot of pride in the things he believes in. He's fair—I don't think he's an unfair kind of competitor. I don't think he'd hop on somebody just because he's the big fellow on the block. He'd knock your head off if you really went up nose to nose with him if he could. If you got a piece of the action, at the same time, there's room for other people. He's not so proprietary. Even though he started the business, he doesn't feel like other people can't get some of the business that he started.

The way I got associated with him, I bought this company here. I bought a major interest in this company that was a competitor of his ten years ago. One of the first things I did was to go around and meet some of my competitors. Ed was the first one I called on. He was very gracious.

Says RAY LEISNER, financial counselor

I think (the secret of his success) is a mixture of opportunity, need in the marketplace of a product and the particular makeup of an individual, psychological and cultural. Ed started an industry, not just a product. He came along at the right time when something was needed. You could call that luck—I call that skill to develop the opportunity that luck may have presented. He saw the need for a better product for the litter box and reacted. I think the biggest single thing that he did was to plough the resources back into the company and to go vertical and to buy the mines and develop the manufacturing process and later on to take it into the supermarkets which required another large capital outlay. Ed has always had the ability and guts to back up his success by leaving his winnings in and pushing them back into the game and directing how they were to be used in a very astute way.

Says DOUG WYANT, extended family member

"He's almost fanatical about being neat," said Mr. Wyant, pointing out a company policy at Lowe's for all employees to leave their work space tidy at the end of each work day.

Mrs. Wyant, who worked in the clerical department for the company recalls that nothing could be left out on a desk top overnight, all desks had to be completely cleared off.

While such rules would seem to suggest a tyrannical type of leadership, Lowe's approachable and personable interest in each employee represented another genuine side of Lowe's personality.

According to Mr. Wyant, if Lowe had a concern or a question about any aspect of the business he'd go straight to the source instead of going through a departmental supervisor.

"And if the tractor guy has a problem he can come right to Lowe," said Mr. Wyant. "He doesn't follow the organizational chain of command and this can throw the whole system off."

Says BRUCE CARLSON, ad agency CEO

(Some of the factors that contributed to Ed's success) One of the things that I think that's always astounded me about Ed is just his basic energy level. I think you can be brilliant as Ed is, be street smart—you can have all those other inherent capabilities if you will, but

if you don't have that energy level to keep driving and keep moving forward, I don't think you could get to where Ed has gotten to. If there is any one thing that helps perpetuate all that he's done, I think its been his energy level. I think there's certain inborn intuitiveness that has to be there.

Says JAN W. ZUPNICK, institute president

I can't answer for how he built Kitty Litter because I've only known him for six years. There are certain qualities which he has that have certainly contributed to what he has done. In my opinion, first of all, he's a person of vision. His whole concept for the American Academy is one, as I've told him I know of no other business man or entrepreneur in the country who has that kind of vision. The word vision and the idea of creating something from nothing and be the first one on the block to do it, had to contribute to the success of his business. Secondly, I have found him to be consistently dogged about wanting to accomplish his vision or the dream. Thirdly, he has sought repeatedly the best professional and other advice to assist him in implementing what he wants to achieve. All those things that contribute to most business ownership success. The special thing I see about Ed is his ability to see things other people don't see and to make money out of it.

I think Ed would have been a successful business person regardless of whether or not he had discovered Kitty Litter.

Says FRANK MORELAND, plant manager

I can't speak too highly of him. I don't know of anything seriously wrong. In 1965 he made me plant manager and told me to put that plant back together. The first thing he did was to tell me to raise everyone 50 cents an hour across the board. Nobody told him to do it. He said they couldn't live on what they had been making. They doubled the damn production in the plant. A few weeks later he wanted to take care of their clothes. Let's put a smile on their wives' faces. Put uniforms on all of them. The women didn't have to launder their clothes. A few months later he said they had to wear hard-toe shoes. He paid for them. There was no union negotiation. He did that of his own free will. That plant jumped up—production doubled. He didn't have to do that. There was nothing made him do that. He reaped the benefits and reward of it.

He's a very fine human. One of the most human business people I know of.

Says EDWIN DARBY, financial editor

(Formerly financial editor and previously Time Magazine's White House correspondent and chief Midwest correspondent for Time and Fortune Magazines.)

Darby: "I thought he (Lowe) was great. I talked to him for hours. I may have written the first thing that was ever written about him on a major publication basis. He was just well started the first time I talked to him. He was not much beyond the point when he took his clay around in paper bags—that's how he really got off the ground. He put a label on them and took them around to cat shows. And he'd sell it in the aisles to individuals and the breeders and the kennel operators. He'd load up his car and take off.

"The last time I talked to him he was traveling in his own private railroad car. And he has a sense of humor. In his place on the near north side, he told me, he had one of these old gasoline pumps from the 1930's and for purposes of parties he would fill it up with Martinis which I thought was great. Another thing about his sense of humor that says something about the man was his purchase of that town, Jones, in Michigan I thought that was a delightful thing, to try to put it back together again the way it was, and he wanted to make a little money along with it by making it a tourist attraction. I thought that was a delightful mindset for him.

Says KENNY HAINES, former employee

I think Ed's interest in the outdoors got him into it. He really loved to be out in the open air and actually bought it as some woodland, just a place to kind of escape and be away from the bustle of the business and it developed from a tract of woods and a cabin to what it is today. He got cleared land, bought a few cows and decided if he was going to have cattle he wanted to have good cattle, and that's what got him into the registered business. He had a good herd of cattle. Then his interest went other ways as well as mine and he got out of that business and continued on with what he's doing there now. The farm is growing in size. I guess its up close to 3,000 acres.

Ed's really a unique fellow, I think. I learned a lot from him and enjoyed my time with him.

Says JERRY BURNS, food broker

One interesting experience with Ed Lowe was his dynamic presentation of Kitty Litter. At one of the sales meetings in Cassopolis, Michigan, he really with a lot of emotion demonstrated the fact that the product is dust free, he really was bringing home the point in relationship to some of the other brands that were claiming to be dust free. The reason it was so memorable is you could just feel the emotion and caring of the man and it came through that whole sales operation.

That's the emotional part of the man, the feeling and the care of his product and what he stands behind, his integrity.

As a person and businessman, he is very smart and perceptive. A lot of people in life will have opportunities to invent a product and that opportunity will come and obviously in his case he recognized the need for a product that would serve as a cat litter.

Says CARMEN ELIO, Boston consultant

I think with Ed, he was successful at what he was doing but he always had an open mind for what other people were doing. Because he was always trying to improve what he was doing. He was always trying to make it better and I think that's the mark of success. Success is always to be better at what you do, to be the best there is. I think you see it in athletes, I think you see it in businessmen and I know you see it in Ed Lowe. He's got vision, he's willing to work hard, and he wants to be the best at what he does.

His mother and dad had the ability to live a good life, hard-working people, and he had an ability to have a business there with them, but he took the risk of saying, gee, this is something I think I can make happen and that was a lucky thing that this woman asked him about it, but he seized on that opportunity. He got it together and went on the road and started selling what was really clay in bags. And he created something out of that.

Says BILLY EDD WHEELER, songwriter

I don't think Ed is a one-dimensional person. He's multidimensional. His interests are many and varied. As I told you earlier, I think he has a great sense of humor. I've told you earlier, I've never been in business with him but I would imagine him to be a very fine businessman because he works hard. He would honor any promise he made. He would fulfill his obligations and he would expect you to do the same. To me Ed is as American as hot dogs and baseball. He's patriotic. He stands for a lot of the best things in America. People who roll up their sleeves and pitch in and do a good job. It was a pleasure to be around Ed all that time because he embodies so many things that I admire. That is, he's the epitome of the work ethic of America and I have this philosophy also that if you work hard you can't help but succeed in whatever field you're in.

Says MARSH BLACKBURN, food broker

I've had the opportunity to see Ed in a lot of different lights and in many different challenging situations. He was the type of leader who really outran his associates and he did so through challenges, perseverance. He left a very large wake in

his trail as he moved along. That's not a negative, it's just a fact. He had a great inner challenge and that inner challenge was very difficult sometimes for his associates to execute and it certainly drove the company forward. I'm sure there are others in the cat litter business or absorbent business who feel as though they were there before Ed. The realities really are that across the country it was Ed Lowe who made the cat litter business what it is today.

Says JACK RAND, geologist

What do I think were some of the factors that led to his spectacular achievement in forming an industrial empire and becoming one of the wealthiest men in america?

I don't know—hard work, energy, get up and go. We'd start early in the morning and go late at night. He didn't stop when I was with him. When he wanted to do something, he'd do it. I think it's just pretty much the huge energy that he has. He could see what was right and what was wrong or who was a fake and who wasn't a fake or whatever. He got people with him that didn't mind working long hours and cared about what they were doing. I don't really know what makes people tick, but I do know that when I was with him it was a long day. It was fun. He wasn't a hard driver. I never got the feeling that he was driving anybody hard.

A LETTER THAT WILL BRING TEARS TO YOUR EYES
(From an old newsboy who happens to be black)

Dear Mr. Lowe:

I am sorry that I won't be able to see you during my current trip to Cassopolis. I didn't want anything except to see how you were doing. I read your autobiography this summer. I have held off reading it for years because I was afraid that I might learn something about you that I wouldn't like. Instead, I found that I couldn't put the book down! Your book brought back many memories for me. If I had seen you I would have told you how you were such a role model for me when I was a kid and thanked you.

You must remember that you were one of my role models when I was a kid. I delivered newspapers for five years, starting when I was 12 years old. During the winter when I felt that I was going to get frost bit and my toes and fingers were going to fall off, I would remember that Ed Lowe started off delivering ice. It's not where you start from in life that's important, its where you end up. If you look at the genealogy of Jesus in Matthew, you realize that he had both a prostitute and a king in his lineage.

There were many times that I wished that I could have been your son Tom. From my perspective, Tom had the easiest job in the world. He got to work indoors and he never had to get his hands dirty and in addition, he got paid above minimum wage! Tom drove a brand new car in high school, while the rest of us, if we had cars, had to constantly repair them because they were so old.

Since those days, I have decided that perhaps I was better off being Ed Gaskin than Tom Lowe. Since my parents didn't give me an allowance, I had to work odd jobs to earn my spending money. I worked at the ring toss during sidewalk days in Cassopolis, I worked at the Cass Fair. I took down rides. I mowed lawns, I worked for the Village clearing land, I sold golf balls that I found outside of the golf course. I did almost anything to earn a few extra dollars. I would have liked to have learned to play golf like Tom, but I didn't have enough money to purchase golf clubs.

As you remember, I came to you when I was a young teen asking you to help me with starting a comic book business. I appreciated the fact that you took the time to meet with me. I haven't forgot that you tried to help me by looking into the Junior Achievement program.

Anyway, I saved my money. I said to myself that I didn't want to be poor all of my life, so at age 15, I purchased my first stocks. My mother took me to the Merryl Lynch broker in South Bend who let me purchase $100 worth of stocks and didn't charge me a commission in order to help me. I may not have been so driven to work so many jobs had I been able to assume that I would be rich by default.

I remember when you purchased the whole town of Jones. I said to myself, "Ed Lowe just bought an entire town." I thought, perhaps I will come back and purchase Cassopolis one day. Today, I know that that wouldn't be such a good idea or investment. I must say that you were an inspiration in many ways. I have never heard a person say a bad word about you. The worst that I have ever heard about you was from one of your employees who called you cheap. For a person such as yourself to have hundreds of employees and to live in the Cassopolis area for all those years, where everyone knows everything about everybody else, and the worst thing that someone says it that their boss is cheap isn't too bad. I hope that I am able to do as well.

I know that you have donated lots of money to worthy and not so worthy causes and you have always maintained a low key, informal profile. I think that that is good. If I ever become rich, I hope to be like that. I must say that I have less interest in becoming rich now. There are such things as having a good quality of life. I think the person who said the money wasn't everything was right. I am very happily married, my wife and I both have our health, and we have a place to stay.

I must tell you that I have been to the slums of India and worked with Mother Teresa and I have been to small villages in Kenya. For some people being well off is having indoor plumbing. If you talk with people who make $25,000 they will tell you that $100,000 is a lot of money. If you talk with people who make $100,000 they will tell you that $1,000,000 is a lot of money and so it goes. I think that at some point you must say I have enough and anything above this is gravy.

Tom told me a story about how one time I was on your pier and your neighbor complained about you having a black person on your pier. You defended your action as opposed to apologizing for it. This was another thing that impressed me about you. That's why I wrote my last letter. I liked you so much that my biggest concern was that I won't see you in heaven so that we could have a long chat.

I am telling you now how you were an inspiration to me, because if I tell you now you can appreciate it. If I say it at your funeral, it will be a little too late.

I thought of approaching you once or twice in order to get you to invest in a project. I decided against it because I knew that you would then see me like everyone else. I also thought that you had given enough in your example. (P.S. the project got funded anyway and is doing exceptionally well.)

Since I wrote to you last, I must tell you that I am in my second year at MIT's Sloan School of Management. That is suppose to mean that I am smart. However, in my case what it means is that the school needed a little diversity so they let me in. However, I must tell you that out of 400 applications, I came in second in the National Black MBA Association Scholarship contest and received a $4,000 scholarship this summer. So I think I've got this fooling people thing down pretty good.

The last thing that I want to say as I ramble through this letter is thanks for your book of poetry. It arrived on my wedding day and my best man and I had a blast reading it. The problem was that it was volume two or number two and I have wondered how do I obtain the others in the series? Have you published other books besides your life story? How does a person obtain those, is there a catalogue? What do you do at the Ed Lowe Foundation anyway?!!

Anyway, have a great Fall and if you are in the area during Christmas, perhaps we can get together then. If you ever come to Boston again to receive another award, please let me know. My wife and I would love to have you over for dinner or perhaps we could meet for lunch.

In Christ,

Ed Gaskin

LETTER TO AUSTIN

Yep, I'm ready to let you in on another of your granddaddy's money-making "secrets". In my day, a sidewalk salesman had to beat the drum in order to attract customers and sell his wares. The only trick there was to be able to beat the drum.

Today it's called advertising.

A great factor in the growth of my Eddie's business—the Kitty Litter empire—was his knack for effective advertising. That's something a lot of folks don't realize. And there was a good reason for his success in that department.

He started with paper bags and a handwritten message on them. Today, as you know, advertising is a huge operation, involving television, computers, pollsters and lots of highpriced "experts" figuring out which "persuasions" will have some influence on "consumer behavior".

Let me tell you real plainly what Eddie did—his *secret* . Some think it's a matter of genius and it might be—but, buddy, it's not all that complicated...

It all begins with the Golden Rule. I helped teach your grandpa how the Golden Rule works. It calls for treating the other fellow just as good as the way you'd like him to treat you. (You can't go wrong on that principle.)

How did he apply that rule to advertising? *Here's how!* He always looked at his product from the point of view of his customer. What good would it do for the cat? For the cat's owner? And for the home they lived in? That's how he looked at it, and that was his secret. He never fought for sales because it might make him rich. No way. He asked people to buy Kitty Litter *because it would make their lives better.*

That was his formula, Austin, and if you keep it in mind, it will serve you well.

Loveya
Grandpa Huber

WHAT SOME NEWSPAPERS HAVE SAID ABOUT EDWARD LOWE...

South Bend Tribune
Sunday, June 17, 1990

BUSINESS BOOT CAMP
Ed Lowe's gift to America

By PAUL DODSON
Tribune Business Writer

CASSOPOLIS, Mich.—Edward Lowe is putting his heart, soul and personal fortune into an effort to jump-start the Yankee entrepreneurial spirit.

It is his gift to America.

Lowe, who soon will turn 70, is chairman and owner of Edward Lowe Industries Inc., a company with $160 million in annual sales which is famed for its Kitty Litter and other catbox filler products.

The effort to put new life into American entrepreneurism is target-·ing young people. An example of this effort is the Edward Lowe Intern Program, which began this past week at Lowe's Big Rock Valley, a 3,000-acre estate near Cassopolis.

Lowe calls the program "entrepreneur boot camp."

The first class of the intern program includes 11 college students. Ten of the students attend colleges or universities within 75 miles of Cassopolis while one of them is from a school in Arizona.

Christopher Petty, director of the intern program, said Lowe plans to offer four such intern programs a year, with the second beginning in September.

Petty described the program as "a 10-week crash program for people longing to be in business for themselves."

Lowe is committing a pot of money and a lot of his time and the time of his employees to the program. Petty said the first 10-week program will have direct costs of approximately $16,000 per student, for a total of $175,000.

The students are paid $200 per week to attend. Room and board are provided. While at Cassopolis, the students will live in two refurbished railroad boxcars, situated on tracks in a wooded area.

Petty said much of the cost of the program involves hiring top-notch business speakers who will come to Cassopolis to talk with the students.

This reporter accompanied the students on an orientation tour of Big Rock Valley this past Monday. It was a bewildering experience.

Big Rock Valley is the most unusual farm one could find. There are beautiful rolling hills, hayfields, woods with huge hardwood trees, a private lake and numerous old farm buildings meticulously restored. Intermixed with all this natural and old-fashioned stuff are ultra-modern facilities and the playthings of a very rich man.

For example, one of Lowe's projects involves breeding pure black quarterhorses. The horses are magnificent.

There is also an 1880-era Quaker meeting house that was moved to the farm from several miles away. In another part of the farm is Billieville, a slice of restored Americana representing a little village of a bygone era. Lowe and his wife, Darlene, also have one of their homes on the property.

Midway through the orientation session, Lowe hosted the students at a picnic held on top of a big hill, overlooking miles and miles of countryside. The hill is the high spot in Lowe's Pickle Barrel Golf Course, another one of his playthings.

The pickle barrels serve as targets for plunking golf balls.

Lowe said he is launching this alternative business education program because he believes there is a need to do things differently than in other business schools.

"The business schools teach management. We're going to teach leadership. They emphasize tactics rather than principles. They value results more than how you get there," said Lowe.

Lowe said there are only two things one can do for entrepreneurs.

"You can run an entrepreneur crisis center. This is where you keep your checkbook on the night stand, ready for the calls from entrepreneurs in trouble—people who can't meet their payroll or buy the raw materials to fill an order. You'll get lots of calls, but there is little you can do except throw money after dreams gone sour.

"Or you can grow'em. That's what we're going to do," said Lowe.

A problem with most business education programs, Lowe said, is that they are being taught by "professors teaching something they know nothing about." His alternative education program will rely heavily on having successful business people, and, in some cases, serve as mentors to help them succeed over a long period of time.

Speaking of the intern program, Lowe said, "There's nothing else like it." He added that he owns 2,000 acres near Arcadia in central Florida. "We could possibly develop another academy down there," he said.

"I love my country but I think America is taking the wrong path." said Lowe. "We are buying certain things overseas and fast becoming a service country. We are losing our manufacturing."

While concerned about America's loss of competitiveness in business. Lowe said he has great hopes for "kids eager to start a business."

Apparently speaking of himself Lowe said, "the persons who have it made, the million-dollar thinkers with entrepreneurial instinct, owe a certain amount to the younger generation to carry it on."

Tribune Business weekly
The Week of July 1, 1992

ED LOWE KNOWS...

The charismatic king of Kitty Litter® has shifted his attention since his 'retirement', and is now dedicated to teaching a generation of budding entrepreneurs where to go

By JAN SPALDING
Tribune Business Weekly

CASSOPOLIS.—In 1974 there were four million cats in America wandering around with no real place to "go." Ed Lowe's invention of clay-based Kitty Litter® and the distribution of it brought kitty out of the cold. In turn, the cat eventually topped the dog as America's pet of choice, exploding the feline population to a count of 20 million today.

Call it poetic justice, but the Lowe Foundation reports there are also four million entrepreneurial businesses operating in the country.

For Lowe, around his Big Rock Valley complex, these budding Rockefellers are pretty cool cats.

And like the cats, without proper resources and with nowhere to go for help, the frustrations these business owners face as they try to succeed in business may leave them scratching at the door.

It may be common knowledge Ed Lowe's latest devotion is to the American entrepreneur, but the extent to which he plans to carry this not so newly found passion is anything but common.

The Edward Lowe Foundation is creating new tools of the trade for entrepreneurialism. With a self contribution valued at $48 million, Lowe has a vision that's on its way to reality.

By using the latest technologies, the foundation is developing innovative educational programs and information services, research and planning tools and support systems directed exclusively at helping the private business owner be more successful.

Lowe sees this population as the keystone of the American free enterprise system—a system which "desperately needs facilities that encourage and educate these owners."

The theory is if you can help entrepreneurs be more successful, you can provide a way to pay back the system of American free enterprise. In other words, if it's strength and vitality you want, strengthen the 80 percent of the American work force working in entrepreneurial businesses, and you'll touch the finances and lives of an incredible number of people.

If the Lowe Foundation can do for American entrepreneurs what Kitty Litter® has done for the American cat, we'll all be witness to one pretty huge ball of yarn.

Entrepreneurs Learning Services

The Ed Lowe mystique consumes the foundation's immaculate 3,000-acre headquarters at Big Rock Valley as well as its core staff of about 10. He's nearly 72, but the man behind the curtain steps out frequently, keeping a tight focus on his investment and its direction.

Within the foundation is the American Academy of Entrepreneurs started in 1989. Many sagas make up the total AAE story, including the combination woodsy/high-tech conference facilities available for management, strategy and leadership type meetings of other not-for-profit organizations.

One of the newest activities is the Entrepreneurs Learning Services, an electronic information network and service center. ELS is an ongoing research effort to remove the obstacles entrepreneurs face in finding information which would help them run their businesses.

Long-term aspirations for the project are spiraling, with the possible creation of a nationally integrated information network already in the making.

Currently, ELS organizes sample business information resources into online, CD-ROM, software, videos, audio tapes, books and handouts, all with the intention of helping entrepreneurs make better decisions by having access to needed information.

"It will share with them the experiences of other successful entrepreneurs and their peers," said Ed Lowe. "This will be one of the main thrusts within the next five years at the foundation."

An integral part of the service is that it is designed specifically for not-for-profit service providers. Its specialized services and exclusive research, therefore, will be saved for the likes of community economic development and small business centers that counsel CEOs and entrepreneurs.

By February of 1991, the foundation had created an operational prototype of an Entrepreneurs Library System—stocked with information thought to be of value to entrepreneurs. In the past year, ELS organizers have worked to identify exactly what information services entrepreneurs would most value and how best to deliver those services to them.

The springboard philosophy

While ELS is being developed as the venue for information, research partnerships with two state universities are serving as providers of that information.

One million dollars in grants for research went to Western Michigan University and Michigan State University departments of business to help develop a profile of the management practices and philosophies of business owners.

Michigan State research concentrated on identifying guiding principles—those elements successful entrepreneurs said contributed to their success. Western Michigan focused on the kinds of problems entrepreneurs have and how they solve them. Some of the problems addressed included severe time constraints, the high rate of divorce among entrepreneurs, personal financial insecurity and the "roller coaster" nature of the entrepreneurial lifestyle.

Over 100 hours of face-to-face interviews with entrepreneurs were video-taped and are being studied.

"So what we have is a series of 'from the horse's mouth,'" Lowe said. "Not academia, not theoreticians, but entrepreneurs talking about their problems and their solutions.

"Essentially that represents a really organized approach to not only what entrepreneurs say, but how they behave and to what they ascribe success," he said. And that will essentially become part of the content for the ELS and the electronic information network.

From county to country

Despite millions of dollars worth of research and technology, it's the networking capacity which gives this ball of yarn its stretch.

The foundation has created a pilot network of the development centers of eight community colleges in southwestern Michigan. By September, each will be hooked by modem to ELS information and its multi-media system.

At Big Rock Valley, this pilot program is seen as the springboard connecting southwestern Michigan to resources throughout the country.

"What you're looking at is the potential for having the same sort of network within the 1,400 or 1,500 community colleges; all of which have business development centers; all of which have a commitment to serve the local economic and entrepreneurial needs of their communities," Lowe said. "And that's exciting."

"If you can create a network of willing local partners who serve local entrepreneurs, you can stand a chance at creating a membership system so that both the service providers and local entrepreneurs of emerging, established and start-up companies could be electronically hooked together."

Although such a connection is still four to five years away, the model is definitely in motion.

TEAM

The fine line between success and failure
Is to know when to hold or to fold,
Is knowing whether a good deal is a good deal
Or one that is laced with Fool's Gold.

In knowing whether the one you are dealing with
Is thinking on both or just one,
Is part of the team, is full of team stream,
Wanting cooperation, success, and fun.

The fine line between success and failure
Is to have that certain rapport
That you see eye to eye — not just pie in the sky
It can open the sturdiest door.

So to those who wish to go it alone,
To those who sit back and dream,
To those, oh, alas, I'll just have to pass.
I take being part of a team.

C'mon team! There's a brick wall just ahead!

How to learn something about yourself

LETTER TO AUSTIN

Hiya Austin! Some more Old Fellow's Talk for you... When my grandson Eddie (your Grandpa Lowe) was a little boy, we had us a saying that went like this: *"Idle hands do the work of the devil."*

His grandma made up another one to go along with that. She used to say: *"A rolling stone gathers no moss, but an empty head draws dust."*

I want you to know right off that little Eddie's hands were never idle, not for a split second. The devil never had a chance with him. His hands were busier than a beehive at honey-making time. And I guarantee you something else—his head was busier than that—no dust cloth was ever needed.

He did 99 things any kid could do, and 100 other things that he thought up on his own. He picked up popsickle sticks every morning, he cracked walnuts, collected stamps and coupons, ran errands and chopped wood. And he managed to have fun, too. He'd play scout in the woods and riverboat captain in the crick. He minded his P's and Q's, and every now and then he'd do his homework. (Not always, mind you, because he might be too busy.)

I notice that some kids like to loaf and laze around, hang about doin' absolutely nothing. The more nothing they do, the better they like it. Grandpa Lowe was cut from a different cloth.

And if anybody asks you why he did so many fantastic things once he was grown up, you tell them it was because he had a headstart on the lazy boys. He was used to doing many, many things, and the momentum never let up.

If they want to know how's come he was so good at hatching brand new ideas? You tell them because there wasn't any dust on his bean.

Loveya
Grandpa Huber

188

THE EDWARD LOWE SELF-EVALUATION

"AM I AN ENTREPRENEUR?"

PROFILE INTERROGATOR

OFFERING SCORED COMPARATIVE VALUES TO INDICATE THE ANSWER

"Entrepreneurs aren't made— they are born.

Many times they don't realize their own potential. This PROFILE INTERROGATOR is to help them recognize themselves, and strengthen their resolve to strike out on their own, rather than waste their time in harnesses that may not fit them."

NOTE

What follows are 93 questions in 9 major categories all relating to characteristics of the entrepreneur. They are multiple-choice questions (offering 278 choices) and the wouldbe entrepreneur should be able to breeze through them with ease...and have fun doing it.

There are no "right" or "wrong" answers. So answer honestly and candidly; the responses are your property and your own business. When you are asked to "pick one" and none of those offered matches your taste *exactly,* pick it, even so. What counts is the comparative value of the choices offered.

You will have fun going through the "Profile" and you will learn more about yourself in so doing. You will be given some interesting choices to make. At the end of it you will find the "SCORING INSTRUCTIONS". These will make the experience even more interesting. Even if your score seems negative, *don't let the final score discourage you.*

Bear in mind how many great actors, after their first audition, were told to go home and be a truckdriver. And how many now-successful writers were told by their teachers, "You don't have the stuff to write." Ed Lowe will remind you, *"If you really want to be an entrepreneur, you will make it. The WILL TO BE is 90% of the game!"*

(Proceed with your responses. Please check each one in its turn before going on.)

PP CATEGORY

PP

1. Which of these flowers is your favorite?
   (PICK ONE)
   - ☒ **A** Rose
   - ☐ **B** Carnation
   - ☐ **C** Orchid

A __|__
B _____
C _____

2. When are you at your mental best?
   (PICK ONE)
   - ☒ **A** Early A.M.
   - ☐ **B** Midday
   - ☐ **C** Late night

A __|__
B _____
C _____

3. How many hours do you like to sleep?
   (PICK ONE)
   - ☐ **A** 8 Max.
   - ☒ **B** 6 Min.
   - ☐ **C** More

A _____
B __|__
C _____

4. Which is your preferred dessert?
   (PICK ONE)
   - ☒ **A** Ice cream
   - ☐ **B** Fresh fruit
   - ☐ **C** Pastry

A _____
B _____
C _____

5. How do you act when exhausted?
   (PICK ONE)
   - ☐ **A** Listless
   - ☒ **B** Cranky
   - ☐ **C** Sleepy

A _____
B _____
C _____

6. How far do you walk on an average day?
   (PICK ONE)
   - ☒ **A** 2 miles
   - ☐ **B** 5 miles
   - ☐ **C** more

A __|__
B _____
C _____

7. Have you ever done any of these?
   (PICK ANY, ALL OR NONE)
   - ☐ **A** Repaired an automobile
   - ☐ **B** Built something with lumber
   - ☐ **C** Written a poem

   A _____
   B _____
   C __2__

8. Which would you rather do?
   (PICK ONE)
   - ☐ **A** Go to a hockey game
   - ☐ **B** Watch football on TV
   - ☐ **C** Go to a movie

   A _____
   B _____
   C _____

9. Which movie star do you admire the most?
   (PICK ONE)
   - ☐ **A** John Wayne
   - ☐ **B** Tom Hanks
   - ☐ **C** Steve Martin

   A _____
   B _____
   C _____

10. Which writer do you like the most?
    (PICK ONE)
    - ☐ **A** Mark Twain
    - ☐ **B** Walt Disney
    - ☐ **C** Mickey Spillane

    A __2__
    B _____
    C _____

11. Which would you rather attend?
    (PICK ONE)
    - ☐ **A** An opera
    - ☐ **B** A tennis match
    - ☐ **C** A musical comedy

    A _____
    B _____
    C __1__

12. On a hot day which would you prefer to drink?
    (PICK ONE)
    - ☐ **A** Lemonade
    - ☐ **B** Beer
    - ☐ **C** Cola

    A _____
    B _____
    C _____

FS CATEGORY

1. Did you know your grandparents?
   - ☐ **A** Yes
   - ☐ **B** No

   FS

   A __2__
   B _____

2. Was your family

(PICK ANY, OR NONE)

☐ **A** Well-off

☐ **B** Poor

☐✗**C** In-between

A _____

B _____

C ___2___

3. Did your parents understand you?

(PICK ONE)

☐ **A** Somewhat

☐✗**B** Not at all

☐ **C** Yes

A _____

B ___2___

C _____

4. What was your father's main occupation?

☐ **A** _____

A _____

5. Did your mother work?

☐ **A** Yes

☐✗**B** No

A _____

B _____

6. Was your care entrusted to a babysitter or a nursery?

☐ **A** Yes

☐ **B** No

A _____

B _____

7. Did you resent this separation from your parents, if it took place?

☐ **A** Yes

☐ **B** No

A _____

B _____

8. Did your parents graduate from high school?

☐✗**A** yes

☐ **B** no

A _____

B _____

9. Did anyone in your immediate family own and run a business?

☐✗**A** Yes

☐ **B** No

A ___3___

B _____

10. What is your family standing?

(PICK ONE)

☐ **A** Only child

☐ **B** Oldest

☐✗**C** In-between

☐ **D** Youngest

A _____

B _____

C ___1___

D _____

CO CATEGORY

1. Do you think the government in Washington is doing:

(PICK ONE)

☐ **A** A good job

☐ **B** An acceptable job

☐ **C** A poor job

CO

A _____

B _____

C _3_

2. The Great Depression occurred in what year-span?

(PICK ONE)

☐ **A** 1920-25

☒ **B** 1930-38

☐ **C** 1940-44

A _____

B _3_

C _____

3. What do the colors of the flag stand for?

(ONE WORD EACH)

☐ **A** Red stands for_____

☐ **B** White stands for_____

☐ **C** Blue stands for_____

A _____

B _____

C _____

4. Which of these Presidents would you have liked to have known?

(PICK ONE)

☐ **A** Carter

☒ **B** Lincoln

☐ **C** Ford

A _____

B _3_

C _____

5. The Fourth of July is a national holiday because:

(PICK ONE)

☐ **A** It was Washington's birthday

☐ **B** It's hot weather vacation time

☒ **C** Our independence was declared on the 4th of July

A _____

B _____

C _____

6. What caused the Great Depression?

(PICK ONE)

☐ **A** Wall Street crash

☐ **B** Unemployment

☒ **C** Lack of purchasing power

A _____

B _____

C _____

7. Who killed President Kennedy?

(PICK ONE)

☒ **A** Oswald

☐ **B** The C.I.A.

☐ **C** Don't know

A _____
B _____
C _____

8. Which of these programs deserves the most improvement now?

(PICK ONE)

☐ **A** Expressways

☐ **B** Postal service

☒ **C** Police

A _____
B _____
C _2_____

9. How would you reduce taxes?

(PICK ONE)

☐ **A** Soak the rich

☐ **B** Reduce welfare

☒ **C** Cut government costs

A _____
B _____
C _4_____

10. Would you like to hold an elective office?

(PICK ONE)

☒ **A** Local only

☐ **B** National

☐ **C** Never

A _2_____
B _____
C _____

CB CATEGORY

1. How did you feel about school?

(PICK ONE)

☐ **A** Hated it

☐ **B** Tolerated it

☒ **C** Liked it

CB

A _____
B _____
C _____

2. Which of these subjects did you like the most?

(PICK ONE)

☐ **A** History

☐ **B** Arithmetic

☒ **C** English

A _____
B _____
C _2_____

3. Do you remember your 4th Grade teacher's name?

☒ **A** Yes

☐ **B** No

A _2_____
B _____

4. What was your scholastic standing?
    (PICK ONE)
    ☐ **A** Top third of class
    ☒ **B** Middle
    ☐ **C** Bottom third

A ____
B __1__
C ____

5. What was your favorite childhood book?
    Name it ___Boxcar Children___

A ____

6. What was your favorite comic strip?
    Name it ___Charlie Brown___

B ____

7. What was your favorite TV Show?
    Name it ___Bewitched___

C ____

8. Did you have any schooling after high school?
    (PICK ANY APPLICABLE)
    ☒ **A** University
    ☐ **B** Trade school
    ☐ **C** Correspondence school

A __1__
B ____
C ____

9. As a child did you...
    (PICK ANY APPLICABLE)
    ☐ **A** Sell newspapers/magazines
    ☐ **B** Run errands for tips
    ☒ **C** Perform chores for allowance
    ☒ **D** Operate your own "business"
    ☐ **E** Collect coupons for prizes

A ____
B ____
C __2__
D __2__
E ____

10. Did you enter any contests?
    ☒ **A** Yes
    ☐ **B** No

A __3__
B ____

11. What games were you good at?
    (PICK ONE)
    ☐ **A** Athletic
    ☐ **B** Spelling bees
    ☒ **C** Card games

A ____
B ____
C ____

12. By the age of 15, what did you want to be when you grew up?
    (PICK ONE)
    ☐ **A** A jet pilot

A ____

☒ **B** A doctor
☐ **C** An engineer

B ____
C ____

MC CATEGORY

MC

1. As a child did you have a nickname?
   (PICK ONE)
   ☒ **A** Yes
   ☐ **B** No
   ☐ **C** Several

A __1__
B ____
C ____

2. What was your greatest drawback as a child?
   (PICK ONE)
   ☐ **A** Too tight discipline
   ☐ **B** Lack of money
   ☒ **C** Loneliness

A ____
B ____
C __3__

3. Did you like and respect your parents?
   (PICK ONE)
   ☐ **A** Yes
   ☐ **B** More or less
   ☒ **C** One or the other

A ____
B ____
C __2__

4. When you were alone as a child, did you:
   (PICK ONE ANY OR ALL)
   ☐ **A** Sing
   ☐ **B** Whistle
   ☒ **C** Play a musical instrument

A ____
B ____
C __1__

5. Were you afraid in the dark?
   (PICK ONE)
   ☐ **A** Yes
   ☐ **B** No
   ☒ **C** Sometimes

A ____
B ____
C __2__

6. Were you afraid of thunder and lightning?
   (PICK ONE)
   ☐ **A** Yes
   ☐ **B** No
   ☒ **C** Sometimes

A ____
B ____
C __1__

7. Were you afraid of heights?

(PICK ONE)

☐ **A** Yes

☐ **B** Not really

☒ **C** Only extremely high

      A _____

      B _____

      C _2_

8. As a child, what was the "naughtiest" offense you were punished for?

☐ **A** Describe _____

      A _____

9. In church or school or at home, were you taught the "Golden Rule"

☒ **A** Yes

☐ **B** No

      A _4_

      B _____

10. What was the happiest year of childhood (from 5 to 15)

A Specify _10_____

      A _____

11. As a child did you belong to:

(PICK ONE, NONE, ANY OR ALL)

☒ **A** Scouts

☒ **B** Choir

☐ **C** Neighborhood gang

☐ **D** Athletic team

☒ **E** Club

☐ **F** None

      A _3_

      B _2_

      C _____

      D _____

      E _1_

      F _____

12. Did you have any pets?

(PICK ONE ANY OR SPECIFY OTHER)

☐ **A** Dog

☐ **B** Cat

☐ **C** Bird

☐ **D** Horse

☐ **E** Other _____

      A _____

      B _____

      C _____

      D _____

      E _____

LA CATEGORY

1. Which of these types do you admire most?

(PICK ONE)

☐ **A** Star athlete

☐ **B** Movie star

☐ **C** Government official

      LA

      A _____

      B _____

      C _____

2. Which of these universities would you rather have a degree from?

(PICK ONE)

- ☐ **A** Harvard
- ☒ **B** Notre Dame
- ☐ **C** Vanderbilt

A _____
B _3_
C _____

3. Would you rather own a:

(PICK ONE)

- ☒ **A** Lear jet
- ☐ **B** Yacht
- ☐ **C** Ferrari

A _2_
B _____
C _____

4. Which of these clans would you prefer to be a member of?

(PICK ONE)

- ☐ **A** The Jackson family
- ☒ **B** The Rockefeller family
- ☐ **C** The Kennedy family

A _____
B _/_
C _____

5. Did you ever consider being a vegetarian?

- ☐ **A** Yes
- ☒ **B** No

A _____
B _____

6. At what age did you break away from the family nest?

A Specify __18_____

A _____
B _____

7. Were you married when you made the move?

- ☐ **A** Yes
- ☒ **B** No

A _____
B _____

8. Did your family object to your move?

(PICK ONE)

- ☐ **A** Yes
- ☐ **B** No
- ☒ **C** Mildly

A _____
B _____
C _/_

9. Who are your greatest cheerleaders?

(PICK ONE)

- ☐ **A** Family
- ☒ **B** Friends
- ☐ **C** Others

A _____
B _/_
C _____

10. Do you think you are capable of becoming "Big Time" in any field?

   ☒ **A** Yes   A ___4___

   ☐ **B** No   B _____

CT CATEGORY

CT

1. What are your three favorite words?

   A 1. _____truTH_____   A __2__

   B 2. _____LOVE_____   B __2__

   C 3. _____GIOD | LORD_____   C __2__

2. Can you think of a word to rhyme with "orange"?

   A Specify _____   A _____

3. Write a 4-line poem about Buffalo Bill, starting with this line as given:

   1. Buffalo Bill was a scout, of course

   A 2. _____who rode upon_____   A __2__

   B 3. _____his horse_____   B __2__

   C. 4. _____all day long_____   C __2__

4. Make up a brand-new word to serve as a name for a revolutionary coffee-maker

   A Specify _____GIOOD MORNING_____   A __3__

5. Are you more at home with:

   (PICK ONE)

   ☐ **A** Graphic art   A _____

   ☒ **B** Music   B _____

   ☐ **C** Drama   C _____

6. Which would you enjoy more:

   (PICK ONE)

   ☐ **A** An art gallery   A _____

   ☐ **B** A rock and roll concert   B _____

   ☒ **C** A ballroom dance   C __2__

7. Take these elements: 3 sticks like this ▬ ▬ ▬ 2 triangles of this size △ △ One 0. (you may add 2 zeroes, if you choose, and one more stick.) WITH THESE ELEMENTS, IN THE BOX DRAW A PICTURE OF ANYTHING:

5

DE CATEGORY

1. Which of these definitions best describes your impression of what an "Entrepreneur" is?

(PICK ONE)

- ☐ **A** Risk-taker
- ☐ **B** Lone Wolf operator
- ☑ **C** An inventive go-getter

2. What quality of yours may qualify you to be an entrepreneur?

(PICK TWO)

- ☑ **A** Intelligence
- ☑ **B** Integrity
- ☐ **C** Imagination
- ☐ **D** Energy
- ☐ **E** Ambition

3. Do you have any qualities such as those you have detected in the writings of Ed Lowe?

- ☑ **A** Yes
- ☐ **B** No

4. If so, which quality seems the strongest?

(PICK ONE)

- ☐ **A** Energy drive
- ☐ **B** Creative enthusiasm
- ☑ **C** Uncommon sense

5. What motivates your desire to be an entrepreneur?

(PICK ONE)

- ☐ **A** To be independent
- ☐ **B** To make a fortune
- ☑ **C** To express myself

6. Would you rather have your company be:

(PICK ONE)

- ☐ **A** Biggest in its field
- ☑ **B** Best of its kind
- ☐ **C** The most profitable

DE	
A	____
B	____
C	_3_
A	_3_
B	_3_
C	____
D	____
E	____
A	_2_
B	____
C	____
A	____
B	____
C	_2_
A	____
B	____
C	_3_
A	____
B	_5_
C	____

7. Which is most important to you:

(PICK ONE)

☒ **A** Your customers'' approval   A _4_

☐ **B** Your stockholders' approval   B _____

☐ **C** Your banker's approval   C _____

8. Would you prefer your management team to be:

(PICK ONE)

☐ **A** Younger than you   A _____

☒ **B** Older than you   B _____

☐ **C** Generally the same age   C _____

9. Do you think business success is due mainly to:

(PICK ONE)

☐ **A** Luck   A _____

☒ **B** Hard work   B _3_

☐ **C** Sufficient money   C _____

10. Do you think your supplier/vendors should:

(PICK ONE)

☐ **A** Contribute to your success   A _____

☒ **B** Help promote your company   B _2_

☐ **C** Mind their own business   C _____

MP CATEGORY

1. Which would you prefer?

(PICK ONE)

☐ **A** Direct customer contact   **MP**

☒ **B** Arm's length contact   A _____

☐ **C** No direct contact   B _____

    C _____

2. Which do you think makes a better incentive program for employees?

(PICK ONE)

☒ **A** Profit-sharing   A _/_

☐ **B** Generous bonuses   B _____

☐ **C** Good pensions   C _____

3. Would you want your computerized accounting system to provide:

(PICK ONE)

☒ **A** Day-by-day details   A _2_

☐ **B** Sound a crisis-alarm   B _____

☐ **C** Reports when ordered   C _____

4. Would you encourage employee suggestions:

(PICK ONE)

☐ **A** On an individual basis   A _____

☒ **B** At regular staff meetings   B __1__

☐ **C** As they offer them   C _____

5. Which employee attribute do you think is most essential?

(PICK ONE)

☒ **A** Loyalty   A __3__

☐ **B** Ability   B _____

☐ **C** Enthusiasm   C _____

6. Which is most important influence in hiring:

(PICK ONE)

☒ **A** Resume & references   A _____

☐ **B** Head hunter selection   B _____

☐ **C** In-person impression   C _____

7. After reading this book, would you enjoy meeting Ed Lowe?

☒ **A** Yes   A __2__

☐ **B** Somewhat   B _____

8. Would you relish a visit to Big Rock Valley or the E&D Cattle Ranch as described in this book?

☐ **A** Yes   A _____

☒ **B** Somewhat   B _____

9. What is the singlemost important thing you have learned from this book?

☐ **A** _____

_____

10. Do you really believe as Ed Lowe believes that the "Don Quixote" spirit can help the independent business person break down the "brick walls" that presently impede us:

☒ **A** Definitely Yes   A __4__

☐ **B** Hopefully Yes   B _____

☐ **C** Doubtful   C _____

(TURN TO THE SCORING INSTRUCTIONS TO GRADE YOURSELF.)

SCORING INSTRUCTIONS

TAKE THE POINTS AS LISTED HERE AND POST THEM IN THE APPRO-
PRIATE BOXES ADJOINING THE QUESTIONS WHERE YOUR RESPONSE
IS MARKED.

*For example: PP1 Shows 2 points for "b" 1 point for "a" and
none for "c". If you picked "a" post the one point in the scoring
column. If you picked "c" post no points. Where no point value is
assigned, pass on to the next number.*

PP CATEGORY (PERSONAL PREFERENCES)

PP1 a=1, b=2 **PP2** a=1 **PP3** a=2, b=1 **PP4** c=3 **PP5** c=2
PP6 a=1, b=2 **PP7** a=2, b=2, c=2 **PP8** a=2, b=1 **PP9** a=2 **PP10** a =2
PP11 b=2, c=1 **PP12** a=1, b=1

FS CATEGORY (FAMILY SITUATION)

FS1 a=2 **FS2** b=2, c=2 **FS3** b=2, c=2 **FS4** **FS5** **FS6** **FS7** a=2
FS8 **FS9** a=3 **FS10** b=1, c=1

CO CATEGORY (CIVIC OPINIONS)

CO1 c-3 **CO2** b=3 **CO3** **CO4** b=3 **CO5** c=3 **CO6** a=1
CO7 b=1, c=2 **CO8** b=2, c=2 **CO9** c=4 **CO10** a=2, c=1

CB CATEGORY (CHILDHOOD BEHAVIOR)

CB1 a=2, b=2 **CB2** a=2, b=1, c=2 **CB3** a=2 **CB4** b=1, c=1 **CB5**
CB6 **CB7** **CB8** a=1, b=2, c=3 **CB9** a=2, b=2, c=2, d=2, e=2
CB10 a=3 **CB11** a=2 **CB12** c=3

MC CATEGORY (MORE CHILDHOOD)

MC1 a=1 **MC2** c=3 **MC3** c=2 **MC4** a=2, b=2, c=1 **MC5** C=2
MC6 c=2 **MC7** c=2 **MC8** **MC9** a=4 **MC10** **MC11** a=3, b=2, c, d=2,
e=1, f. **MC12** a=2, b=2, c=1, d=2, e.

LA CATEGORY (LIFE AMBITIONS)

LA1 a=2 **LA2** b=3 **LA3** a=2 **LA4** b=1 **LA5** a=1 **LA6** **LA7** a=2
LA8 c=1 **LA9** b=1 **LA10** a=4

CT CATEGORY (CREATIVE TALENTS)

CT1 a=2, b=2, c=2 **CT2** a=2 **CT3** a=2, b=2, c=2 **CT4** a=3 **CT5** a=2
CT6 c=2 **CT7** (any drawing at all)=5

DE CATEGORY (DEFINING ENTREPRENEUR)

DE1 c=3 **DE2** a=3, b=3, c=4, d=4, c=4 **DE3** a=2 **DE4** a=2, b=3, c=2
DE5 a=2, c=3 **DE6** b=5, c=2 **DE7** a=4 **DE8** a=3 **DE9** b=3
DE10 a=4, b=2

MP CATEGORY (MANAGEMENT PHILOSOPHY)

MP1 a=3, **MP2** a=1, b=3, c=2 **MP3** a=2, c=1 **MP4** a=2, b=1
MP5 a=3, b=1, c=2 **MP6** c=2 **MP7** a=2 **MP8** a=2 **MP9**
MP10 a=4, b=2

Now tally up the score you have posted, adding all the points registered to the choices you made.

THE SCORE BOARD

A NATURAL: If you have tallied more than 178 you may well be a ripe candidate for entrepreneurism.

A POSSIBLE: If you score is less than 115 but more than 80 you are certainly eligible to try your hand at entrepreneurism.

FORGET IT: If you ended up with fewer than 70 points, you probably should try for a job with some big corporation.

A LAST REMINDER

THIS IS ONLY AN "INDICATION" AND MAY WELL BE IN ERROR. YOUR "WILL TO SUCCEED" IS MORE IMPORTANT THAN ANY TEST SUCH AS THIS.

PLEASE:

When you have scored yourself, will you drop me a line (letter, post card or fax) to tell me:

- What your score was and what it means to you.
- Where the test was confusing or unfair in your opinion.
- What you liked about the book as a whole.
- Most important thing you learned from the book.
- Any negative reactions you might have.

I'd like to hear from you!

Edward Lowe
Big Rock Valley
Cassopolis, MI 49031

HAIL TO YOU!
Entrepreneurs-in-need and
Potential Entrepreneurs

A PERSONAL STATEMENT
BY THE AUTHOR

Now that you have read my book, please understand me when I tell you—*I wrote this book for you!*

Each and every chapter and verse may not be tailor-made for you specifically, but if you are in the fast lane of an independent business operation (or trying to get in it) *then the bulk of what I've written here should serve you well.* I sincerely hope so.

When I was selling my KITTY LITTER I made a point to tell my customers: "I LOVE YOUR CAT". Now let me bring that up-to-date:

"FELLOW ENTREPRENEUR, I LOVE YOU!"

...Believe me, and if you, in your turn, love your country and believe in Tomorrow, then I know America will be in good hands.

Edward Lowe

THE END